Survival from the Fittest: A companion cookbook to *Survival for the Fittest* from the athletes of the AIS, has been produced in association with Nestlé Australia Ltd.
ABN 77 000 011 316

First published in 2001 by
Murdoch Magazines Pty Ltd (Custom Books division)
Pier 8/9, 23 Hickson Road
Millers Point NSW 2000

Murdoch Magazines Pty Ltd. ABN 62 007 619 767

Manager, Custom Books   Nicola Hartley
Custom Books Coordinator Karina Haehnle

Art Director   Melissa Mylchreest
Food Editors   Tracy Rutherford
                 Jody Vassallo
Photographer   Sue Ferris
Food Stylist   Patrick Collins

The authors would like to thank Katrina Koutoulas, Karen Taylor and Nicola Hartley for their assistance with *Survival from the Fittest*. We also thank Susan Wright for making it happen in the first place.

We thank the athletes who provided recipes and quotes for this book. Involvement in this project does not imply support of any commercial product or association with the AIS or Nestlé Australia Ltd.

Sports images supplied by the Australian Sports Commission, Australian Institute of Sport, Department of Sports Nutrition and featured athletes. Selected sports images on inside front cover, rear inside cover and pages 29, 52, 75, 79 courtesy ALLSPORT. Sports image on page 26, courtesy Tony Palmer, News Limited. Sports image on page 68, courtesy Ansett Collection, Australian Sports Commission. Sports image on page 71, courtesy Randy Stenglein. Sports image on page 76, courtesy GL Photography.
© 2001 food photography and design Nestlé Australia Ltd

This edition printed by Tien Wah Press, Singapore

Distributed by Allen & Unwin
83 Alexander Street, St Leonards NSW 2065

National Library of Australia Cataloguing-in-Publication Data
Survival from the fittest : companion cookbook to *Survival for the fittest* from athletes at AIS.

Includes index.
ISBN 1 876652 48 9.

1. Athletes — Nutrition. 2. Low-fat diet — Recipes.
3. High-carbohydrate diet — Recipes. I. Burke, Louise.
II. Australian Institute of Sport.

AUSTRALIAN
SPORTS
COMMISSION

survival
FROM THE FITTEST

**AUSTRALIAN
INSTITUTE OF SPORT**

about this book

At the Australian Institute of Sport, we were overwhelmed by the response to our first cookbook *Survival for the Fittest*. Our athletes loved it, and it was a bestseller in the general community. We realised that we had struck a chord with active people who want simple, healthy and tasty meals, as well as with young people who are developing the skills for domestic success. The first cookbook, "Survival 1", added pizzazz to AIS cooking classes, and inspired the athletes to push their performances in the kitchen, as well as in the competition arena. It didn't take long before they started to campaign for another book.

Many of the AIS athletes wanted to contribute their own favourite recipes to a new book. Others wanted us to take their favourite meal ideas or cooking styles and remodel them into lean and streamlined recipes. The bottom line was to join forces and share their knowledge of eating for success.

As in the first book, we recognise that the cutting edge in sports nutrition can't be achieved by athletes without organisation and skill in the practical sides of preparing meals. We also recognise the challenges of being an athlete – being tired or overcommitted, and having to take responsibility at an early age. Although their food must meet the nutritional profile required to underpin training and competition goals, athletes still want meals to taste delicious and they want to be part of social eating occasions with friends and family. This second book, *Survival from the Fittest*, goes even further to deliver recipes and cooking tips for non-elite chefs straight from the mouths of some of Australia's most dedicated and successful athletes.

contents

eating for endurance

Eating to train

- Distance runners, swimmers, rowers, cyclists and triathletes have demanding training schedules with long, moderate to high intensity sessions, which mean a high energy and carbohydrate bill. Refuelling between sessions is vital—inadequate carbohydrate intake leads to depletion of muscle fuel stores, causing fatigue and ineffective training.
- Low body-fat levels are valuable in sports if athletes have to move their own body mass over long distances or against gravity, since it lightens the 'dead weight'. Some athletes are excessive in their strategies to become light and lean. The key is to find a body-fat level that is consistent with good health and performance in the long term. Severe restriction of energy intake and dietary variety can lead to fatigue, nutritional deficiencies, hormonal imbalances, and disordered and unenjoyable eating.
- Although the focus is on fuel foods, endurance athletes also have increased needs for protein and various vitamins and minerals. They are often at risk of poor iron status, due to the combination of a low intake of readily absorbed iron and increased iron losses. Iron deficiency is another cause of fatigue and poor recovery.
- Healthy bones need an environment of exercise, adequate calcium and hormonal balance. Menstrual dysfunction in female athletes impairs bone health—the immediate problem may be stress fracture, but in the long term there is an increased risk of earlier onset of osteoporosis. All athletes must eat high-calcium foods. Females should seek immediate help with menstrual irregularities.
- Lengthy work-outs mean high sweat losses, especially during hot weather. Without a fluid intake plan, it is easy to become chronically dehydrated.

Eating to win

- The main fatigue factors during prolonged events are dehydration and depletion of carbohydrate fuel stores. Strategies for eating before, during and after the event are important to reduce the impact of these factors.
- When competition involves multiple stages or a series of heats and finals, recovery between sessions is an important factor in determining the ultimate winner.

Nutrition Strategies

1. Meals should be based on carbohydrate-rich foods. Our recipes cater for athletes with high fuel needs, and mix and match nutritious fuel foods with protein sources, and fruits and vegetables. This ensures that athletes achieve their nutrient needs, and enjoy a range of foods.
2. Athletes with very high energy and fuel needs will require the larger portion serves of our recipes at meals, as well as snacks and action-packed fluids between meals. Desserts can be enjoyed after meals, or as supper.
3. Key strategies for athletes working toward lighter and leaner shapes include low-fat eating and attention to serve sizes. The smaller portion serve of our recipes may be sufficient, with plenty of salad and vegetables. Fruit, yogurt or hot chocolate are light choices to finish meals, with desserts as occasional treats. Well-placed snacks help to prevent hunger or overeating at the next meal.
4. Fluid and fuel needs are key issues in competition, and in long events there is opportunity to refuel and rehydrate 'on the run'. Sports drinks provide an ideal balance of fluid and carbohydrate to look after both needs simultaneously, and are designed to taste good. Develop a fluid intake plan, using opportunities in your event to replace as much sweat loss as practical. In very long events, such as triathlons, use sports bars, gels and other carbohydrate foods for variety and extra fuel. Practise your strategies in training to promote better performance during sessions and fine-tune tactics for competition.
5. It is important to recover quickly after training sessions or multiple-stage competition events and prepare for optimal performance in the next work-out. Substantial refuelling can only occur after carbohydrates are eaten, so have a fuel-rich snack or meal soon after the session. While some athletes can eat a high-carbohydrate meal within 30 minutes of the end of a work-out, others are challenged by isolated locations or by fatigue and poor appetite. A snack providing 50-100 g of carbohydrate starts the refuelling process until you're ready to eat your next meal. Many snacks can also provide other nutrients which may be important in repair and adaptation.
6. Even with good strategies, most endurance athletes are in fluid deficit at the end of a training session. You can't rely on thirst to promote rehydration, so monitor your body weight before and after the session instead. In general, you should drink enough to replace 150 per cent of the post-event fluid deficit (e.g. drink 3 litres of fluid to replace a 2-litre or 2-kg weight loss). After all, sweat and urine losses will continue before fluid balance is achieved. Since sweat contains sodium and other electrolytes, athletes who incur large sweat losses in a session must actively replace sodium during recovery. The everyday diet generally contains more than enough sodium for this, but, between two training sessions or competition stages, you may need sodium-containing foods such as sports drink, bread, breakfast cereal, or savoury, salted foods.

---

50 G CARBOHYDRATE SNACKS

- 600-800 ml sports drink
- 500 ml soft drink or fruit juice
- 2 carbohydrate gels
- 1 large bread roll with banana filling
- 1 jam or honey sandwich + 250 ml sports drink
- 80 g chocolate bar or jellybeans
- 2 cereal bars + 1 piece of fruit
- 60 g (1-2 cups) breakfast cereal + 200 g NESTLÉ Light Fruit Yogurt*
- 250-350 ml liquid meal supplement or fruit smoothie*
- 1 ham or cheese sandwich + 250 ml fruit juice*
- 60 g sports bar + 250 ml sports drink*
- 1 cup creamed rice + 1 piece of fruit*

*These choices are also good sources of protein and some micronutrients.

---

eating for team sports

Eating to train

- Football, basketball, netball, volleyball and hockey are seasonal sports. At the recreational level, the off-season can be lengthy and many players lose fitness and gain body fat as a result of detraining and poor eating practices. This may also occur with injured players during the season. Since it may take many weeks or most of the pre-season to get back into shape, team-sport players should eat well and keep active year round.

- At the elite level, most players train year round, with a brief break between seasons. Most competitions involve weekly games, with players undertaking team and individual training sessions in between matches. Re-fuelling is an important part of recovery between matches, and for keeping up with the weekly training schedule. Traditionally, many team-sport players have turned to high-carbohydrate eating only on the night before a match, or in the pre-event meal. However, the daily demands of training and competition are best met by a permanent approach to an adequate fuel intake.

- Games and training are often held in the late afternoon or evening, interfering with the traditional dinner meal.

- Physique plays an important role in the performance of some sporting codes, or positions within the same code. Team-sport players often have special nutritional needs to support rapid growth spurts, or the goals of intensive weight-training programs. Protein needs are often emphasised, but, in fact, total energy and fuel needs are of primary importance, as well as increased requirements for some vitamins and minerals.

- Large fluid losses during training sessions often go unrecognised—especially in winter-based team sports. The tradition of 'toughening up' players by not drinking during a work-out is an unfortunate remnant from 'the old days'. High-intensity play creates sweat losses, which can be increased by heavy clothing and protective gear, or indoor arenas with poor air circulation. Of course, sweat losses are further increased in hot weather.

Eating to win

- Depletion of muscle glycogen stores can be a source of fatigue in team games that are longer than 60 minutes—especially for players who get a lot of playing time and have a mobile position or game style. Studies show that high-carbohydrate eating strategies, such as fuelling up in the days before a match or consuming carbohydrate (sports drink) during a match, can enhance performance of these players. For example, it may allow them to run further and faster in the second half of the match and make less mistakes in skill and judgement.

- Rehydration is another proactive nutrition strategy for team sports.

- A weekly match schedule calls for active recovery techniques, and demands are even greater in tournaments where teams play each day or every second day for a week or fortnight leading up to a grand final. When full recovery of fuel and fluid balance isn't possible between games, the benefits of consuming fluid and carbohydrate during the match are even greater.

Nutrition Strategies

Team-sport players should utilise Nutrition Strategies 1–6 in Eating for Endurance (see page 6), but the following strategies are also of value.

1. When training and game schedules interfere with the daily eating routine, adopt a new meal plan. Some players reorganise their day to eat their main meal at lunch, then refuel after a late work-out with a quickly prepared but substantial snack. Others have a meal prepared, which can be 'zapped' when they get home. Many of our recipes are 'one-pot meals' suitable for freezing or refrigerating, and reheating in minutes.

2. The pre-event meal is a good opportunity for a shared meal, ensuring all players undertake their final nutritional preparation well and providing a good opportunity to boost morale and share final tactics. Depending on the match time, many of our high-carbohydrate recipes can be adapted to provide players with a variety of high-fuel choices.

3. Most team sports offer opportunities for players to refuel and rehydrate during the game, including time-outs, substitutions, and formal quarter-time and half-time breaks. Some sports even allow trainers to carry drinks onto the playing arena during breaks in play. Players should actively make use of these opportunities, and consume a sports drink to look after both fluid and carbohydrate needs.

4. Post-game recovery is another good time for a team nutrition plan. Alcohol is often a part of post-game activities in team sports, but should be discouraged until recovery nutrition goals are achieved. Even then, players who choose to drink alcohol should do so in moderation. Post-game snacks or a team meal, providing nutrient-rich, high-carbohydrate choices and rehydration drinks, will help players to achieve their recovery needs while celebrating or commiserating the results of the game.

IDEAS FOR PRE-MATCH MEALS –
HIGH-CARBOHYDRATE CHOICES
- Breakfast cereal + low-fat milk and fruit
- Muffins or crumpets + jam or honey
- Pancakes + syrup
- Toast + baked beans or tinned spaghetti
- Creamed rice
- Rolls or sandwiches with banana filling
- Sandwiches with lean meat or cheese + salad fillings
- Fruit salad with low-fat fruit yogurt
- Pasta with tomato or other low-fat sauces
- Risotto or rice dishes with low-fat ingredients
- Baked potatoes with low-fat filling
- Sports bars or cereal bars + sports drink
- Fruit smoothie (fruit + low-fat milk + yogurt or ice cream)
- Liquid meal supplement

eating for strength and power

Eating to train and win

- Sprinters and field athletes, weightlifters, powerlifters and body builders aim to gain strength, and often size, through specially designed weight-training programs. When increases in muscle size and strength are required, most athletes focus on protein needs. In fact, apart from genetic potential and the right training program, an essential ingredient is adequate energy intake, which includes special needs for protein, carbohydrate and micronutrients.

- Some power athletes also need to consider weight and body fat goals, especially lifters who compete in weight divisions and body builders who are judged according to their lean and 'ripped' appearance. Shedding kilograms and body fat is an activity associated with competition preparation, and is often taken to extremes in the days or weeks prior to the event. Instead, the power athlete should take a long-term approach to their ideal physique, achieving a safe and sensible level in training that is close to competition goals. Competition preparation should require only a fine-tuning effort.

- Training sessions are best undertaken when the athlete is well hydrated and well fuelled. Often, power athletes forget about these nutritional needs, and fail to bring a drink bottle to training. Fuelling with a sports drink can help to keep the athlete lifting or training with good technique right to the end of the session.

- Post-training recovery is an important goal for power athletes. A snack providing a combination of carbohydrate and protein, with fluid to rehydrate, is the perfect approach. Some recent evidence suggests that it's even better to have this recovery snack just before the weight-training session.

- The sports world is filled with supplements that promote better recovery, faster muscle gains from training, increased fat loss, and enhanced performance. These claims are attractive to all athletes, but seem particularly connected to the world of strength training and body building. Since the supplement industry is loosely regulated, it is easy for manufacturers to make false or exaggerated claims about products.

Nutrition Strategies

1. Power and strength athletes require meal plans based on carbohydrate-rich foods to fuel training, and plenty of protein, vitamins and minerals to build the results. The recipes in this book have been developed to achieve good carbohydrate and protein combinations.

2. Athletes who need additional energy to make gains in body size and muscle strength will need the larger portion serves of our recipes at meals, as well as snacks and action-packed fluids, such as fruit smoothies, between meals. A cooked or prepared dessert can be enjoyed after meals, or as a late supper before bed.

3. Key strategies for athletes working towards lighter and leaner shapes include low-fat eating, and paying attention to serve sizes. These are discussed in greater detail in Nutrition Strategies in Eating for Skill and Agility (see page 9).

4. A few supplements and sports foods provide good value and real enhancements to the athlete's training and competition program. However, for independent and up-to-date advice about what really works and how to make best use of it, consult a sports dietitian.

IDEAS FOR HIGH-ENERGY SNACKS – NUTRITIOUS CHOICES RICH IN CARBOHYDRATE AND PROTEIN
- Fruit smoothies or liquid meal supplements
- Sandwiches or toasted sandwiches
- Fruit salad + NESTI F l ight Fruit Yogurt
- Sports bars + fruit juice or sports drink
- Creamed rice
- Muffins, scones or fruit buns + flavoured milk
- Fruit-and-nut snack mix + fruit juice or sports drink

eating for skill and agility

Eating to train and win

- It takes a lot of practice to develop skill. Archers, shooters, golfers, gymnasts, figure skaters and divers train for many hours each day for many years to develop their talents. Some athletes may include specialised conditioning such as weight training to develop their strength. Despite the length of training sessions and the involvement of high-intensity activities, the overall energy cost of training may be low to moderate.

- As a result of low-moderate training costs, and the lack of time for other activities, skill and agility athletes may get less assistance from their training to remain in shape. Some archers, shooters and golfers can be overweight by population standards and need to lose body fat for health benefits. In gymnastics, skating and diving, the athlete may struggle to achieve and maintain the lean and petite physique that is 'de rigueur' for the skills and aesthetics of their sport.

- When skill athletes reduce their food intake to meet their lower energy needs, they need to choose nutrient-rich foods to ensure that they meet fuel requirements for training as well as special needs for vitamins and minerals. In some cases, for example, female athletes with delayed onset of puberty and menstruation, needs for minerals such as calcium are increased.

- Skills and concentration are marred by dehydration and fuel depletion.

Nutrition Strategies

1. The recipes in this book are based on carbohydrate-rich, moderate-fat eating. When restricting energy intake to stay trim, the athlete should look for recipes that are gold medal winners for calcium and iron, and with plenty of vegetables, to ensure that nutrient needs are met from the small-portion serves.

2. The skill athlete should keep well fuelled with carbohydrate-rich choices before competition and training sessions. During lengthy sessions, particularly in the heat, fluids should be consumed to promote hydration. When long exercise sessions result in skipped meals, a carbohydrate-rich snack or carbohydrate drink should be consumed to refuel.

IDEAS FOR STAYING LEAN AND TRIM
- Don't overdo the portion size at meals. Choose the smaller serve size of recipes, and fill the plate with extra vegetables or salad.
- Have a well-chosen snack in the afternoon to prevent extreme hunger at night. Don't snack between meals for entertainment rather than need. If you like to have something before bed, save something from your dinner rather than having extra food.
- Choose low-fat cooking methods, as used in these recipes. Avoid adding butter, margarine, cream, oils or creamy dressings to foods.
- Choose lean cuts of meat, fish and poultry, and remove skin and fat before cooking.
- Try low-fat versions of dairy foods, and use cheese (even the reduced-fat types) as a sprinkle rather than in slabs.

how the fit survive ~ the skills & challenges

Getting on top of the shopping and cooking is not hard and the pay-offs of good eating are great. Here we've listed some key strategies and tips.

Where Possible, Use Teamwork

■ If you share a house, call a team meeting to organise for tasks to be shared. When time or money is scarce, it helps to pool resources.

■ Don't worry if conflicting timetables mean you only meet up a few times a week. Use your time together to plan and roster the tasks of shopping or cooking. Use lists to communicate what is needed.

■ Use your rest day to do shopping and cooking tasks that help other housemates. You will be pleased to enjoy the same assistance on your busy days.

Acquire New Skills

■ Gradually master new cooking skills. Use recipes in this book to learn a style of cooking (e.g. a risotto or a stirfry), then branch out on your own by changing a few ingredients. Practice makes perfect!

■ Collect tips from other athletes or good cooks. Adapt information from various sources to suit your needs.

Plan Ahead and Manage Your Time Well

■ Start with a well-organised and clean kitchen. This makes cooking quick and easy.

■ Make a list of basic items for the freezer, fridge and pantry, and always keep these in stock. Note when stocks are running low, and take advantage of supermarket specials to grab multiples of these items.

■ Plan your meals for the week ahead and note the required ingredients. Make a shopping list from this and add your general food-stock needs.

■ Avoid supermarkets in peak hours. Shop late or early to help save time.

■ Avoid shopping when you're hungry or tired — the shopping list is likely to go out the window.

■ Only buy products that you can use within their use-by date. Choose good-quality products that have been appropriately stored.

■ Plan your meals to take advantage of leftovers or batch cooking. For example, if you are having rice as an accompaniment one night, cook extra to make into fried rice on the following evening. Pasta sauces can be served on the next night as a potato filling.

■ Use rest days to cook ahead for the week. Make one or two dishes that can be refrigerated or frozen. It's great when you come home late and tired from training to find that the hard work has been done.

■ Even if you're cooking for just one or two people, make the whole recipe to ensure leftovers and save you from cooking again the next night. (Cook double quantities if you are feeding a few.) You can also freeze leftovers in single-size portions, to thaw or reheat as required. Invest in a good set of clear plastic containers that you can label and stack in the freezer.

■ Prepare as much of the recipe as you can before going to training (e.g. make the pasta sauce or chop the ingredients for a stirfry), as this speeds up the cooking process when you get home.

■ Plan snacks that can be eaten on the run or taken with you on a busy day—for example, single-serve cereals, cartons of yogurt, cereal bars, fruit, and even leftovers.

■ Make up a loaf of sandwiches when you have roast meat or deli meats on hand. Meat or cheese sandwiches freeze well, and can have salad added when thawed.

Using Creative Shortcuts

- Invest in a few good cooking tools or household items that save time and produce quality outcomes. A good wok, large nonstick frying pan, microwave oven, sharp knives, lasagne dish and pizza trays (and cutter) are all good purchases. A rice cooker may also be useful.
- Make use of nutritious time-saver products available in supermarkets. There are many that make good meals, or form the base for cooking a meal quickly (see list).
- It sometimes helps to buy meat already trimmed or diced for a stirfry, or frozen and fresh vegetable stirfry mixes. They can cost a little extra, but often the time you save in meal preparation is worth this expense.
- Soften hard vegetables, such as potato, pumpkin and carrots, that need to be chopped and cooked by microwaving for 1–2 minutes to make them easier to cut.
- Leftover rice and pasta can be frozen. To reheat, microwave or pour boiling water over it and drain.

- If you haven't got time to cook rice or pasta with a meal, use couscous. It can be prepared in minutes.
- Fresh pasta cooks more quickly than dried varieties. Gnocchi cooks in a minute, while fresh lasagne sheets cut the baking time in half.
- If you are not adventurous with flavouring dishes, make use of prepared pasta and stirfry sauces and even fresh soups. These can be used as the flavouring base of a dish to which you add your own choice of meat and vegetables.
- Jars of minced herbs provide authentic flavour and save you having to chop or grate items such as garlic or ginger and waste the unused portions. Some fresh herbs, for example, parsley or coriander, are worth buying and you can also freeze them in small portions for later use.
- Be versatile. Know which ingredients are vital for a recipe and which can be replaced easily. Exchange recipe items with what you have in your fridge or pantry or according to which foods are in season or 'on special' in the supermarket.
- Choose recipes that are complete meals for single-portion freezing. If the dish is self-contained with meat, vegetables and a carbohydrate choice, you will need no meal preparation other than reheating or you may even be able to eat it straight from the container.

vegetarian corner

The vegetarian recipes in *Survival from the Fittest* have been designed to provide nutritious, complete meal ideas. Even if you're not vegetarian, branch out to try these recipes and learn how to use meat alternatives to create a delicious and nutrient-packed meal.

In general, a vegetarian diet can support optimal sports performance. Studies have demonstrated that a well-chosen vegetarian diet contains adequate protein, is high in carbohydrate and low in fat—ideal for athletes striving to meet dietary guidelines for sport. The key issue for athletes who are vegetarian or near-vegetarian is to explore alternatives to replace the nutrients normally provided by meat.

Some athletes adopt a vegetarian diet to meet increased carbohydrate requirements for training or to assist in weight control. This is commonly seen among endurance athletes such as runners, cyclists and triathletes—athletes who have a daily challenge to refuel, yet stay lean. However, the focus of vegetarian eating is not simply replacing the meat, chicken and/or fish at meals with extra vegetables. Instead, strategies need to be found to replace the energy, protein, iron and zinc which are typically found in animal-derived foods with a vegetarian alternative.

Nutrition Tips for Vegetarians

- Make sure you eat a variety of food choices, including protein-rich and carbohydrate-rich foods at each meal. Vegetarian sources of protein and minerals include lentils, dried beans and peas (ready-to-use products are available), tofu, tempeh, textured vegetable (or soy) protein, and ready-made nut, soy or wheat-derived meat alternatives. Many supermarkets now stock vegetarian versions of 'mince', 'sausages' or 'luncheon meats' ('salami' or 'ham').
- You may need help to experiment with vegetarian meat alternatives. Specialist vegetarian cookbooks can provide recipe ideas and special tips for cooking with legumes, soy and other meat alternatives.
- If you have recently converted to a vegetarian diet, you may find that you lose more weight than is desirable. This is a common result when bulky, high-fibre foods such as beans and legumes are used as a replacement for meat, chicken and fish. Athletes in heavy training or undergoing growth spurts have very high energy requirements. It is sometimes difficult to eat enough when meals are based on bulky food that requires lots of chewing. In this situation, it is good to find more compact and energy-dense vegetarian foods—for example, gluten meat alternatives, textured vegetable protein, tempeh, tofu, fruit juices, dried fruits, nuts, peanut or nut butter, honey and jams. For lacto-ovo vegetarians, low-fat milk, reduced-fat cheese and other low-fat dairy products are also low in bulk and energy-dense.
- Make sure you include protein-rich foods at meals, especially at the midday meal. Many lacto-ovo vegetarians use cheese as a convenient meat alternative, whereas vegans may fail to use suitable protein alternatives. As an athlete you may have limited time for meal preparation, particularly at lunch. Convenient meat alternatives for lunch include ready-prepared beans (e.g. baked beans), nut and seed spreads (such as peanut butter, tahini and almond spread), and ready-made luncheon meats, derived from wheat gluten.
- If you use soy milk instead of dairy milk, choose a calcium-fortified option since many soy milks are low in calcium. Read the nutrition analysis panel and choose a soy milk that contains at least 100 mg of calcium per 100 ml of fluid. If you don't drink dairy milk or a calcium-fortified soy milk, other suitable non-dairy calcium-rich alternatives include tofu, soy yogurt and soy custard. Breakfast cereal and low-oxalate green vegetables such as broccoli and bok choy also provide calcium, but it is important to have a daily eating plan that provides at least three serves of calcium-rich foods. For most people, calcium-rich milk, yogurt and cheese are the easiest foods to include in basic eating plans.
- For strict vegan athletes, vitamin B12 deficiency is a primary concern. Dairy foods and eggs provide sufficient vitamin B12 for lacto-ovo vegetarian athletes, but vegan athletes must consume a known source of vitamin B12 such as fortified soy milks, or consider vitamin B12 supplementation. Dietary intake of riboflavin may also be limited for vegan athletes, particularly those who avoid soy milk and soy milk products. Rich sources of riboflavin include fortified breakfast cereal, grains, textured vegetable proteins, soy milk, yogurt, custard and cheese, and yeast-extract spreads such as Marmite™ and Vegemite™.
- It is common practice for some athletes to take iron supplements in fear of having low iron levels. Taking iron supplements is only warranted where iron depletion or iron-deficiency anaemia has been diagnosed by a doctor. There are two forms of iron in the diet—haem iron which is found in animal-derived foods such as red meat, chicken, liver and eggs; and non-haem iron which is found in breakfast cereal, bread, legumes, nuts and green leafy vegetables. Non-haem iron sources are poorly absorbed by the body, so it is important for vegetarians to recognise iron-rich foods and factors that inhibit or enhance iron absorption. The best sources of iron in a vegetarian diet include breakfast cereal (especially those commercially fortified with iron—check the nutrition information panel), bread, textured vegetable proteins, legumes, dried beans, gluten-based vegetarian meat alternatives, nuts, dried fruits and green leafy vegetables. Include a rich source of vitamin C, such as orange juice or salad, with your meals to enhance the absorption of iron.
- Although a vegetarian diet is inherently low in fat, you should still be aware of high-fat foods in your diet. Consuming large amounts of full-fat dairy products and adding excess amounts of extra fats, oils and salad

dressings will increase the amount of fat in your diet. In this book, we have developed recipes based on low-fat dairy foods and soy alternatives, low-fat cooking methods, and vegetarian meat alternatives.

- The Australian Vegetarian Society produces a quarterly journal, *New Vegetarian and Natural Health*, which contains reliable nutrition education messages, suitable vegetarian recipes and details of vegetarian meeting groups and restaurants throughout Australia. The current website address for the Australian Vegetarian Society is: www.moreinfo.com.au/avs.

Other good vegetarian websites include:

- The International Vegetarian Union (www.ivu.org) has a comprehensive website that also provides links to the vegetarian societies throughout the world.
- The Vegetarian Resource Group at www.vrg.org.
- Sanitarium Health Food company at www.sanitarium.com.au.
- The Vegan Society, based in the United Kingdom, at www.vegansociety.com.

Cooking Tips for Vegetarians

- Many traditional meat dishes can be easily converted into vegetarian dishes. Mince is easily replaced in recipes by using either brown or green lentils or textured vegetable protein. Try the vegetable lasagne on page 55 to see how easy it is to use textured vegetable protein in a recipe.
- Tofu is a great substitute for chicken in most recipes. Although some people complain that tofu is bland and tasteless, there are many seasoned options on the market. You can also season tofu yourself, prior to cooking. Spray a frying pan with an oil spray, add garlic, ginger, soy sauce and sweet chilli sauce. Add the tofu, turning frequently, and cook until browned. You can use this seasoned tofu, for example, to replace the pork on page 80.
- Tofu can also be marinated or coated in spices. Cut the tofu into 1-cm slices and marinate in plum sauce, soy sauce and garlic. This is absolutely delicious when barbecued and served on a crusty bread roll with salad.
- Don't be deterred by recipes which use beef or chicken stock—use vegetable stock instead. NESTLÉ produce a ready-made MAGGI All Natural Vegetable liquid stock.
- When using textured vegetable protein in a wet dish such as pasta sauce, don't rehydrate it before use. To cut down on preparation time, simply add it straight to the recipe with extra liquid (the textured vegetable protein will absorb some of the liquid from the dish).
- Nutmeat is a great substitute for beef in a stirfry. Simply slice the nutmeat then cut into cubes. As nutmeat is a pre-cooked meat alternative, it should be added at the end of the recipe cooking time.
- Canned lentils, kidney beans and three-bean mixes are nutritious options that are great to use in cooking. If you have the time to soak them, dried lentils and beans are cheaper options. However, canned options definitely decrease the recipe preparation time. They are found in the canned vegetable aisle in the supermarket.
- If you are soaking dried lentils or beans, make a double batch and freeze half. They keep for up to three months.
- Vegetarian sausage rolls are delicious and easy dinner party starters which can be made quickly from a packet of vegetarian hotdogs and a packet of puff pastry, look for lower fat versions. Allow the pastry sheets to thaw, then roll out with a rolling pin to spread the pastry further. Cut the pastry to fit—1 sheet when cut should wrap 4 hotdogs. Wrap the hotdogs in the pastry and then cut each one into thirds. Place on a greased baking tray, make a couple of slices diagonally across the top of each bite-sized sausage roll, and brush with low-fat milk. Bake in a preheated hot oven until brown on top. Serve with tomato sauce and sweet chilli sauce.
- The health-food section of most supermarkets usually provides an excellent array of vegetarian food options. Also check the fridge section for fresh tofu, vegetarian sausages and luncheon 'meat' slices.

how to use this book

Consider this book as a stepping stone towards great cooking. We hope that it will help you gain the confidence to become a winner in the kitchen. The recipes we have chosen were developed or adapted from AIS recipes to include most of the following features:

- Delicious taste
- High in carbohydrate for fuel and low in fat to keep you in shape
- Quick to prepare and cook—typically able to be on the table in 20-40 minutes
- A meal in one pot—a good balance of fuel, protein, and vitamins and minerals in the one dish
- Basic techniques with few pots and pans to clean up
- Good for leftovers or for freezing as a self-contained meal

We have also tried to use commonly found ingredients, and on occasions to take advantage of some convenience food products. The recipes demonstrate cooking techniques that can be applied in other settings, so we recommend you learn to experiment with them using our tips or suggestions for ingredient substitutes as a guide.

There is no such thing as a typical athlete. In suggesting serve sizes, we have generally catered for athletes with medium energy needs (4 serves to a recipe) and athletes with lesser energy needs (6 serves to a recipe). Nutrition information for each recipe is provided for these typical serve sizes. However, we all know athletes who have huge energy needs, and it is possible that two of these athletes will eat a whole dish between them. Therefore, interpret the nutrition information with your needs in mind.

The following information is provided about each recipe:

- ENERGY VALUE
  Although people think of energy as 'get up and go', in fact it is simply the kilojoule (kJ) or calorie (Cal) content of the food
- CARBOHYDRATE CONTENT
  Provided as grams (g) per serve
- PROTEIN CONTENT
  Provided as grams (g) per serve
- FAT CONTENT
  Provided as grams (g) per serve
- Special comments ~ These may note content of fibre, iron, calcium, vitamin C or zinc.

Medals Scheme

Our system of medals helps you to analyse the nutrient content of a meal and whether or not it is likely to help you meet your nutrition goals. The medals take into account the overall picture of a winning diet, and the role each recipe is likely to play.

- Gold   A real winner
- Silver   Nearly there
- Bronze   Needs a little more work

Other Symbols

✳   Good for freezing

This symbol means that the recipe is suitable for freezing. Freeze the whole amount in an airtight container, or better still, divide it into single serves which can be quickly thawed and heated as required. Most meals can be left in the freezer for up to 2-3 months.

COOKING GOURMET MEALS

Most of the time, athletes want to eat no-fuss, quick and healthy meals, but there may also be occasions when you want to entertain others or take a little more time and trouble with the meal preparation. Many of the recipes in this book are suitable for dinner parties and entertaining. With a little extra care, you can ensure your guests are impressed by your culinary skills.

- Use all fresh ingredients such as fresh herbs, fresh seafood or fish, and fresh vegetables.
- Take time to cut vegetables into attractive shapes, such as long thin strips.
- Use nice plates and bowls to enhance the presentation of meals, and set the table artistically to create the scene.
- Show flair when serving pasta sauces, risottos or stirfries. Rather than mixing or tossing all the ingredients together, serve the pasta, rice or noodles on the bowl or plate, then arrange the meat and vegetables in a colourful design on top.
- Use fresh garnishes such as parsley, dill, coriander or other herbs. Experiment with more exotic varieties of your favourites, such as flat-leaf (Italian) parsley or gourmet lettuce mixes.

oven-baked chips

creamy cucumber dip

thorpie's fruity salsa dip

spicy tomato salsa

➤ To make low-fat mayonnaise: place 1 can condensed skim milk and 200 ml white vinegar mixed with 1-2 teaspoons mustard powder into a large screw-top jar and shake to mix. Leave to stand until thickened.

➤ Using 1 cup low-fat mayonnaise or natural yogurt as a base, make seafood-style sauce by adding 2 tablespoons tomato sauce and 1 teaspoon Worcestershire sauce. For a tartare-style, add chopped capers, a dash of lemon juice and chopped fresh parsley if desired.

➤ For an avocado-based dip: mash 1 avocado and mix with 1 cup natural yogurt or ricotta cheese. To spice it up, add a dash of lemon juice, tomato salsa, onion or chilli to taste.

➤ To make low-fat potato wedges: cut potatoes into wedges, place in a microwave-proof bag, and cook on HIGH for 3-5 minutes, or until softened. Remove wedges from bag, place on a nonstick baking tray, and spray lightly with oil. Season if desired with paprika, chilli powder or dried herbs. Bake wedges in a preheated 200ºC (400ºF) oven for 15-20 minutes, or until golden brown. Turn wedges during baking so they cook evenly. The longer you cook them, the crunchier they are.

➤ Starters are great when matched with meals—for example, yogurt and mint dip before curries, or refried bean salsa and a sprinkle of cheese before Mexican-style food.

---

thorpie's sweet crisps Serves 2-4

1 tablespoon lemon juice
1 tablespoon caster sugar
$1/2$ teaspoon ground cinnamon
3 sheets lavash bread

Preheat oven to 190ºC (375ºF). Put lemon juice in a small bowl, and combine sugar and cinnamon in another bowl. Brush the bread (wholemeal if you like) lightly with juice, then sprinkle with sugar mixture. Cut bread into 3 strips lengthways, and 4 pieces crossways. Cut each piece in half diagonally to make triangles. Place on baking trays, and bake for 8 minutes, until crisp. Serve with Thorpie's Fruity Salsa Dip.

Preparation time: 10 minutes
Cooking time: 8 minutes

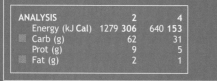

ANALYSIS	2		4	
Energy (kJ Cal)	1279	306	640	153
Carb (g)		62		31
Prot (g)		9		5
Fat (g)		2		1

---

starters

Starters are a great way to begin meals—whether for yourself or your guests. They're quick to make, and can be nibbled when you're hungry and preparing your food.

The range of ideas for starters is virtually unlimited, however, they can very easily become a high-fat trap that unbalances a healthy meal and leaves little room for more nutritious food. High-fat, low-carbohydrate starters to avoid include traditional fatty dips, cheese, deli meats, any food marinated in oil or fried, pâtés and pastry.

Healthy Dips / Although some commercial dips are high in fat, there are also many low-fat varieties. You can easily make your own low-fat dips by adding flavours to a low-fat base—natural yogurt (low-fat, 1% fat; regular, 4% fat); ricotta cheese (low-fat, 3–5% fat; regular, 11% fat); cottage cheese (6% fat); extra light sour cream (12% fat); homemade mayonnaise (0.1% fat) [see Hints & Tips]; avocado with yogurt or ricotta cheese (12% fat); salsa (0% fat); refried beans (1% fat).

Compare these healthy bases with traditional dip ingredients: cream cheese (33% fat), sour cream (36% fat), cream (35–45% fat) and mayonnaise (70–80% fat).

Add flavour to dip bases with ingredients such as sauces (tomato, Thai sweet chilli, barbecue, oyster, mushroom, kecap manis, soy, teriyaki, relish, chutney); spices (Cajun, tandoori, Thai, satay, garam masala); minced herbs (garlic, basil, coriander, ginger, chilli, mint); pickles or sundried tomatoes; grated vegetables (carrot, beetroot); creamed corn or corn kernels.

Dippers / There's a great variety of dippers to go with low-fat dips, including fresh fruit and vegetables in bite-sized pieces; rice crackers, pretzels and other low-fat crackers such as water crackers; flatbread, poppadoms, rye or pumpernickel bread; and potato wedges (see Hints & Tips). To make your own pitta chips, spray pitta bread with oil and bake in a preheated hot oven for 10 minutes, or until golden brown. Flavour the pitta before baking with herbs and spices for savoury dips or with sugar for sweet dips, if desired.

oven-baked chips Serves 2-4

olive or canola oil spray
2 potatoes, 250 g each, scrubbed clean (Desirees are good for chips) or 500 g
sweet potato (these won't be as crispy)

Preheat oven to 230°C (450°F). Lightly spray 2 large baking trays with oil. Cut
potatoes into even, thin slices (about 3 mm thick). Place on trays in a single layer.
Spray lightly with oil. Bake for 25–30 minutes, until crisp and golden brown.
Depending on the oven, you may need to swap trays around halfway through
cooking. The chips may stick to the trays, so lift them off using a butter knife. Serve with dip. Season with sea salt if desired.

ANALYSIS	2	4
Energy (kJ Cal)	895 214	448 107
Carb (g)	33	17
Prot (g)	6	3
Fat (g)	6	3
Vitamin C		

Preparation time: 10 minutes
Cooking time: 30 minutes

creamy cucumber dip Serves 2-4

2 small Lebanese cucumbers
2 teaspoons minced garlic
1 cup PETERS FARM No Fat Natural Yogurt
2 teaspoons chopped fresh mint

Peel cucumbers and cut in half lengthways. Use a teaspoon to scoop out the seeds.
Grate the flesh, and place in a bowl with garlic, yogurt and mint. Stir to combine and serve chilled. Season with freshly ground black pepper and garnish with chervil if desired. Makes about 1½ cups.

ANALYSIS	2	4
Energy (kJ Cal)	348 83	174 42
Carb (g)	10	5
Prot (g)	8	4
Fat (g)	<1	<1
Calcium		

Preparation time: 5 minutes
Cooking time: Nil

thorpie's fruity salsa dip Serves 2-4

1 large mango
1 punnet strawberries, washed and hulled
2 kiwifruit, peeled
pulp of 2 passionfruit
1 tablespoon shredded fresh mint
2 tablespoons apricot jam

Cut the cheeks from mango, and peel. Chop fruit into small even-sized pieces and
place in serving bowls. In a small bowl, combine passionfruit, mint and jam. Add to fruit and stir gently to combine. Serve with Thorpie's Sweet Crisps (see Hints & Tips).

ANALYSIS	2	4
Energy (kJ Cal)	815 195	407 97
Carb (g)	42	21
Prot (g)	5	2
Fat (g)	<1	<1
Fibre, Vitamin C		

Preparation time: 15 minutes
Cooking time: Nil

spicy tomato salsa Serves 2-4

4 ripe tomatoes, finely chopped
1 teaspoon finely chopped fresh red chilli
½ small red onion, thinly sliced
½ cup fresh coriander leaves
2 teaspoons lime or lemon juice

ANALYSIS	2	4
Energy (kJ Cal)	230 55	115 27
Carb (g)	8	4
Prot (g)	4	2
Fat (g)	<1	<1
Vitamin C		

Put all ingredients in a bowl and stir to combine. Makes about 2 cups.

Preparation time: 10 minutes
Cooking time: Nil

IAN THORPE ~ swimming
thorpie's fruity salsa dip
Greatest sporting achievement:
The Sydney 2000 Olympics —
including 3 gold medals in the
4 x 100m relay, 4 x 200m relay,
and 400m freestyle.
Favourite food:
My mother's baked dinner —
it's the best thing about coming
home from overseas.
My contribution to Survival 2:
This salsa is light and great for
summer — and so easy to make.
I first tried it at a friend's place
in the USA, then worked on the
recipe to perfect it.

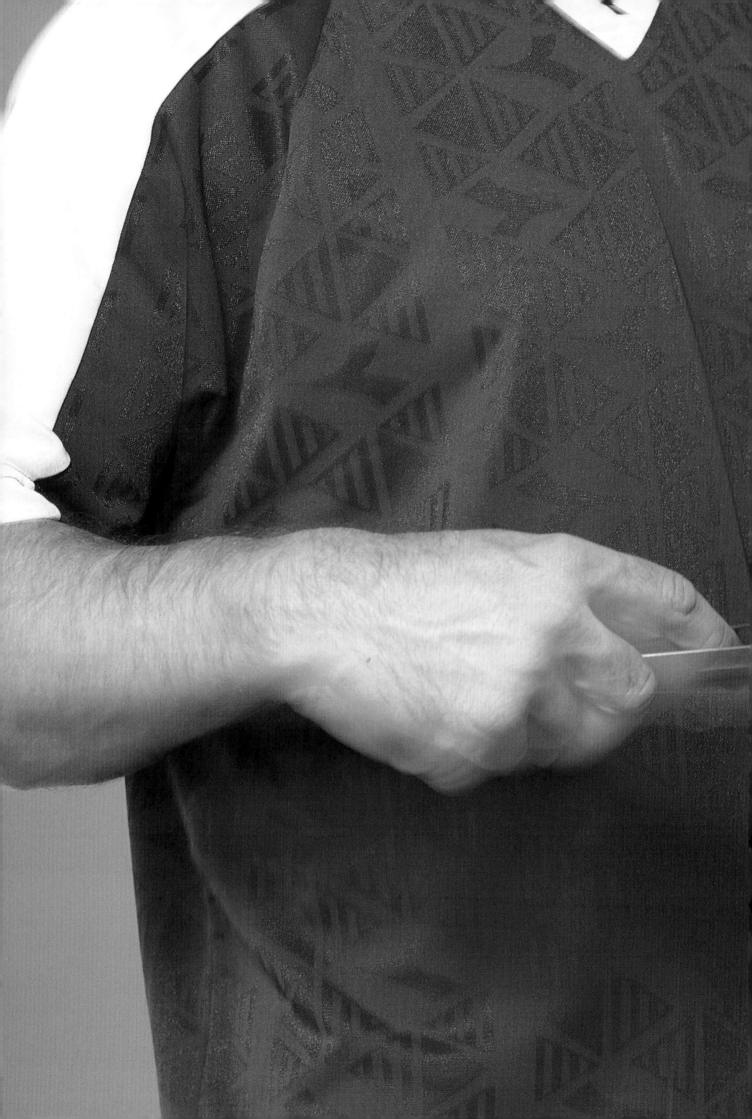

soups&salads

soups & salads

Soup and salad meals are often undervalued as sources of fuel for athletes, and traditional recipes can be loaded with fat and short on carbohydrate. With a little bit of planning, however, these starters can be highly nutritious and easily transformed into a satisfying main meal.

Hearty soups full of potato, pasta or grains like rice and barley provide a burst of carbohydrate to refuel the hungry and tired athlete. A soup full of different-coloured vegetables also provides antioxidant vitamins and minerals. Serving bread with soup boosts its refuelling power and forms a perfect partnership, so we've made suggestions to go with our recipes.

Salads can range from a few 'greens' to accompany a meal or cleanse the palate, to the more substantial ones that are meals in themselves and a great source of many antioxidant vitamins and minerals. To make the most of them, leafy salads should be consumed with other foods to ensure adequate intake of carbohydrate and protein. Better still, create complete salads based on high-carbohydrate foods such as pasta, noodles, rice or potato and experiment with grains like polenta, couscous and burghul.

The choice of dressings is critical to ensure that salads are nutritious meals. Creamy dressings are loaded with fat and it is easy to add large amounts which unbalance the goodness provided by the salad. Use a dash of a good-quality oil or commercial dressings in fat-free or low-fat varieties—these are bursting with flavour so you don't have to compromise on taste when dressing your salads. Do be careful, however, with reduced-fat or cholesterol-free commercial salad dressings. Check the nutrition panel on the label, and keep below 20 grams of fat added to a 4-serve salad.

Legumes and pulses such as soy beans, kidney beans, chickpeas or commercially available bean mixes also make great additions to soups and salads. These are high in carbohydrate, protein and fibre, whilst being low in fat, and they are also a rich source of vitamins and minerals, antioxidants and phyto-oestrogens.

sweet potato soup

sweet potato soup   Serves 4-6 ❊

olive or canola oil spray
1 large onion, chopped
2 teaspoons minced garlic
1 teaspoon minced chilli
2 teaspoons ground coriander
1 kg sweet potato, peeled, cut into small cubes
1 litre MAGGI All Natural Chicken or Vegetable Liquid Stock
150 ml can CARNATION Light and Creamy Evaporated Milk
½ cup chopped fresh coriander leaves
4 small crusty loaves, such as mini cobs

Spray a large saucepan with oil and heat. Cook onion over medium heat for 3–4 minutes, until soft. Add garlic, chilli and ground coriander, cook, stirring, for 1 minute. Add sweet potato and chicken or vegetable stock. Bring to the boil, then reduce heat and simmer, partially covered, for 20 minutes, until sweet potato is tender. Cool slightly and purée in a blender until smooth. Return to the saucepan, add milk and reheat gently. Stir through coriander and garnish with extra whole leaves if desired. Serving suggestion: Slice the top off the cobs. Scoop out chunks of bread from the inside to make a well, but leave a small amount attached to the crust. Bake cobs in a preheated 210°C (415°F) oven for 5–7 minutes until the crust is crisp. Place cobs on serving plates, ladle soup into them, and sprinkle with fresh coriander. Arrange cob "lid" and bread chunks around the cob, as soft croutons. Eat the cob "bowl" after the soup. Serve with salad.

ANALYSIS		4		6
Energy (kJ Cal)	2109	504	1406	336
▪ Carb (g)		91		61
▪ Prot (g)		22		15
▪ Fat (g)		6		4
▪ Fibre, Vitamin C				
▪ Calcium, Iron, Zinc				

Preparation time: 15 minutes
Cooking time: 30 minutes

chicken & vegetable laksa-style soup   Serves 4-6 ❊

TARYN LANGDON ~ rowing
chicken & vegetable
laksa-style soup
Greatest sporting achievement:
I'm still waiting for that one.
Ask me again in a few years.
Favourite part about Survival I:
The chocolate brownies recipe.
Who said healthy food can't
taste good?
My contribution to Survival 2:
I love my laksa, and we don't
have it in the Dining Hall.
I wanted a healthy recipe, quick
to cook with the authentic taste
of a laksa. So here it is!

olive or canola oil spray
½ small red onion, finely chopped
2 teaspoons finely chopped lemongrass
1 teaspoon finely chopped fresh red chilli
1 teaspoon minced ginger
½ teaspoon ground turmeric
1 litre MAGGI All Natural Chicken Liquid Stock
125 g dried rice vermicelli noodles
500 g or 2 skinless chicken breast fillets, halved lengthways and thinly sliced
1 bunch broccolini, cut diagonally into thirds
1 red capsicum, cut into thin strips
1 carrot, cut into thin strips
375 ml can CARNATION Light and Creamy Evaporated Milk
1 teaspoon coconut essence
2 teaspoons MAGGI Fish Sauce
⅓ cup fresh coriander leaves

Spray a large saucepan with oil and heat. Add onion and cook over low heat for 3 minutes, until soft. Add lemongrass, chilli, ginger and turmeric, and cook, stirring, for 30 seconds. Add stock and bring to the boil. Add noodles, chicken and vegetables. Return to the boil, reduce heat to medium-low, and simmer uncovered for 5 minutes, until noodles are soft, vegetables are just tender and chicken is cooked through. Stir in milk with coconut essence and heat through. Stir through fish sauce and serve topped with coriander leaves. Serve with bread.

ANALYSIS (inc. bread)		4		6
Energy (kJ Cal)	2473	591	1649	394
▪ Carb (g)		67		45
▪ Prot (g)		50		33
▪ Fat (g)		13		9
▪ Calcium, Iron, Vitamin C, Zinc				

HINT: *This soup is best served immediately. Vary the recipe with vegetables such as bok choy, zucchini, baby corn or snow peas, or use firm white-fleshed fish fillets instead of chicken.*

Preparation time: 15 minutes
Cooking time: 10 minutes

chicken & vegetable laksa-style soup

thai-style chicken salad

lamb & noodle salad

thai-style chicken salad Serves 4-6

500 g dried rice vermicelli noodles
olive or canola oil spray
500 g or 2 skinless chicken breast fillets, cut into thin strips
2 small mangoes, peeled and sliced
1 punnet cherry tomatoes, quartered
4 spring onions, sliced diagonally
1 Lebanese cucumber, halved lengthways and sliced
2 tablespoons lime or lemon juice
2 tablespoons MAGGI Fish Sauce
1 tablespoon soy sauce
2 tablespoons MAGGI Authentic Thai Sweet Chilli Sauce
1/3 cup fresh coriander leaves
2 tablespoons crushed peanuts, optional
1 small cos lettuce

Cook noodles in a large saucepan of boiling water until tender. Drain, rinse thoroughly with cold water and drain well. Spray a nonstick frying pan with oil and heat. Cook chicken over medium–high heat for about 5 minutes or until browned and cooked through. Place noodles, mango, tomato, spring onion, cucumber and chicken in a bowl. In a small bowl or jug, mix lime juice and sauces. Pour over noodle salad and toss well to combine. Divide among serving plates, and sprinkle with coriander and peanuts. Serve lettuce on the side. Garnish with extra spring onions, if desired.

ANALYSIS	4		6	
Energy (kJ Cal)	2617	625	1745	417
■ Carb (g)		95		64
■ Prot (g)		37		25
■ Fat (g)		10		6
■ Iron, Vitamin C				
■ Zinc				

HINT: *Use the meat from a barbecued chicken, avoiding any skin or fat, instead of breast fillets.*

Preparation time: 20 minutes
Cooking time: 10 minutes

lamb & noodle salad Serves 4-6

Dressing:
185 ml CARNATION Light and Creamy Evaporated Milk
1 teaspoon coconut essence
2 tablespoons reduced-fat peanut butter
1 tablespoon soy sauce
2 tablespoons MAGGI Authentic Thai Sweet Chilli Sauce

olive or canola oil spray
300 g trim lamb fillet
900 g fresh thin hokkien noodles
150 g green beans, cut diagonally into 4-cm lengths
1 small red onion, cut into thin wedges
1 large carrot, halved lengthways, finely sliced diagonally
3 stalks celery, thinly sliced
400 g can baby corn, drained, spears halved lengthways

Place all the dressing ingredients in a small saucepan and stir over low heat until combined. Set aside. Spray a nonstick frying pan with oil and heat. Add lamb and cook for 5 minutes on each side. Transfer to a plate, cover loosely with foil, set aside for 5 minutes, then cut into thin slices. Meanwhile, place noodles in a large heatproof bowl, cover with boiling water. Gently separate the strands using a fork and stand for 5 minutes. Drain well. Place beans in a small heatproof bowl, cover with boiling water, stand for 3 minutes. Drain, rinse under cold water and drain well. Arrange noodles, vegetables and lamb on serving plates, and drizzle with dressing. Garnish with flat-leaf parsley leaves, if desired.

ANALYSIS	4		6	
Energy (kJ Cal)	3708	886	2472	591
■ Carb (g)		147		98
■ Prot (g)		47		31
■ Fat (g)		11		8
■ Fibre, Iron, Zinc				
■ Calcium				

Preparation time: 15 minutes
Cooking time: 10 minutes

AUSTRALIAN AND AIS
Women's Cycling Team
thai-style chicken salad
Favourite part about Survival 1:
We're based in houses in Italy for most of the cycling season, and do all our own cooking. It was great to receive our delivery of the first 'Survival' cookbook. Not only did it remind us of home, it gave us lots of new ideas and recipes to try.
Our contribution to Survival 2:
We like to eat salads for lunch, and they need to be quick and simple to make. With the price of meat in Europe, and the fears of mad cow disease, we focus on chicken and fish. The Thai-style salad is very versatile.

gonzo's baked bean burritos

gonzo's baked bean burritos Serves 4-6 ❄

olive or canola oil spray
450 g can refried beans
2 x 425 g cans of mexe-chilli beans
375 g enchilada sauce
chilli powder (optional)
2 cups cooked rice (brown or long-grain rice is best)
10 burrito tortillas
½ cup grated low-fat tasty cheese
½ iceberg lettuce, shredded
3 carrots, cut into thin strips
4 tomatoes, quartered
2 Lebanese cucumbers, cut into thin strips
alfalfa sprouts

Preheat oven to 180°C (350°F). Lightly spray a large ovenproof dish with oil. Combine refried beans, mexe-chilli beans and half the enchilada sauce in a large mixing bowl. Add a pinch of chilli powder, if desired. Divide both the bean mixture and rice into 10 equal portions. Place a portion of bean mixture across the centre of a tortilla. Place a portion of rice next to the beans, and roll up the tortilla. Place the burrito into prepared dish. Repeat until all tortillas are filled. Pour remaining enchilada sauce over the burritos, and sprinkle with cheese. Bake for 25 minutes, until cheese is melted and golden. Combine remaining ingredients to make a salad. Serve burritos with salad on the side.

ANALYSIS	4		6	
Energy (kJ Cal)	3029	724	2019	482
Carb (g)		122		82
Prot (g)		37		25
Fat (g)		9		6
Calcium, Fibre, Iron, Vitamin C, Zinc				

Preparation time: 15 minutes
Cooking time: 25 minutes

JOHN FORBES ~
tornado catamaran sailing
gonzo's baked bean burritos
Greatest sporting moment:
Winning the under-7 Major and Minor Premiership with my soccer team when I was a kid.
Favourite recipe/cooking style:
Australian—you can't beat an Aussie barbecue with your mates.
My contribution to Survival 2:
I love eating baked beans, even as a snack—I can eat a whole tin, not a problem. The baked bean burritos turn the trusty baked bean into a quick, easy meal that even I know how to cook.

lamb & lentil soup Serves 4-6 ❄

olive or canola oil spray
1 onion, finely chopped
2 teaspoons minced garlic
1 kg butternut pumpkin, peeled and chopped
2 potatoes, peeled and chopped
1 cup red lentils
1 litre MAGGI All Natural Chicken Liquid Stock
4 large silverbeet leaves, chopped
200 g lamb backstrap
freshly ground black pepper, to taste
crusty bread, to serve

Spray a large saucepan with oil and heat. Add onion and cook over medium heat for 2–3 minutes or until soft. Add garlic and cook for 1 minute more. Add pumpkin, potato, lentils and stock. Bring to the boil, reduce heat to low, and cook, covered, for 15 minutes, stirring occasionally. Add the silverbeet and cook another 5 minutes. Meanwhile, spray a nonstick frying pan with oil, and cook the lamb for 5 minutes on each side. Transfer to a plate, cover loosely with foil and stand for 5 minutes. Finely slice the meat across the grain; add to soup and heat through. Season with freshly ground black pepper, and serve with crusty bread. Note: The pumpkin weight is for the whole piece, including skin and seeds.

HINT: *For a vegetarian soup, omit the lamb and use vegetable stock; served with bread, it provides complete protein. This soup will keep for up to 2 days in the fridge, or freeze for up to 2 months. Place individual portions in airtight containers. Thaw frozen portions in the fridge for about 10 hours (transfer from freezer to fridge in the morning to eat that night).*

ANALYSIS	4		6	
Energy (kJ Cal)	2164	517	1443	345
Carb (g)		76		50
Prot (g)		37		25
Fat (g)		8		5
Fibre, Iron, Vitamin C, Zinc				

Preparation time: 15 minutes
Cooking time: 30 minutes

lamb & lentil soup

beef & couscous salad

minestrone by nathan

beef & couscous salad   Serves 4-6

olive or canola oil spray
1 kg butternut pumpkin, peeled, seeded, cut into 2-cm cubes
1 punnet cherry tomatoes, halved
1 bunch asparagus, halved
435 ml MAGGI All Natural Chicken Liquid Stock
2 teaspoons finely grated orange rind
$^{1}/_{4}$ cup orange juice
1 teaspoon minced ginger
2 cups couscous
2 boneless sirloin steaks (about 250 g each), excess fat removed
3 spring onions, sliced
1 bunch rocket

Preheat the oven to 210°C (415°F). Spray an oven tray with oil and arrange pumpkin cubes in a single layer. Bake for 20 minutes, then add tomatoes to the tray and cook a further 10 minutes. Meanwhile, place asparagus in a heatproof bowl and cover with boiling water. Stand for 5 minutes, then drain. Place chicken stock in a large saucepan and bring to the boil. Stir through rind, juice, ginger and couscous, cover tightly with a lid, remove from heat and stand for 5 minutes. Transfer to a large bowl and separate the grains using a fork. Spray a nonstick frying pan with oil, and cook the beef for 8-10 minutes on each side. Transfer to a plate, cover loosely with foil and stand for 5 minutes. Finely slice the meat. Add spring onion, asparagus, pumpkin and tomatoes to the couscous and toss until well combined. Serve with rocket leaves and sliced beef. Garnish with orange zest, if desired. Note: the pumpkin weight is for the whole piece, including the skin and seeds.

ANALYSIS	4		6	
Energy (kJ Cal)	2830	676	1887	451
Carb (g)		96		64
Prot (g)		47		32
Fat (g)		11		7
Iron, Vitamin C, Zinc				

HINT: *This salad is great for summer entertaining. Cook the meat on the barbecue, if desired.*

Preparation time: 20 minutes
Cooking time: 30 minutes

minestrone by nathan   Serves 4-6   ❄

olive or canola oil spray
1 onion, finely chopped
2 rashers bacon, chopped
2 carrots, halved lengthways, thinly sliced
2 zucchini, halved lengthways, thinly sliced
4 ripe tomatoes, chopped
1 litre MAGGI All Natural Chicken or Vegetable Liquid Stock
1 cup small pasta shells
$^{1}/_{2}$ cup frozen green peas, defrosted
400 g can borlotti beans, rinsed and drained
crusty bread, to serve

Spray a large saucepan with oil and heat. Add onion and bacon and cook over medium heat for 5 minutes or until onion is soft and bacon is brown. Add carrot, zucchini, tomato and stock. Bring to the boil, then reduce heat to medium and cook, partially covered, for 5 minutes. Add pasta and cook for 5 minutes, then add peas and beans and cook for another 5 minutes or until the pasta and vegetables are tender. Garnish with flat-leaf parsley leaves, if desired. Serve with crusty bread.

ANALYSIS	4		6	
Energy (kJ Cal)	2374	567	1583	378
Carb (g)		89		59
Prot (g)		28		19
Fat (g)		11		7
Fibre, Vitamin C				
Iron				

HINT: *For a vegetarian soup, omit bacon and use vegetable stock. Also, try other canned beans, such as cannellini or red kidney. This soup is better made a day in advance as the flavours will improve, but only add the pasta when reheating. It keeps for up to 3 days in the fridge.*

Preparation time: 15 minutes
Cooking time: 20 minutes

NATHAN DEAKES ~ race walking
minestrone by nathan
Greatest sporting moment:
6th in 50km walk and 8th in 20km walk at 2000 Olympics.
Food dislikes: Eggplant, pumpkin (although I like pumpkin soup—figure that one out!).
My contribution to Survival 2: Despite participating in Northern Hemisphere racing, I never manage to miss the entire Canberra winter. This minestrone is a great way to keep warm in winter and is absolutely delicious with Italian carbone bread.

split-pea chowder Serves 4-6 ❄

250 g yellow split peas
olive or canola oil spray
1 large onion, finely chopped
2 teaspoons minced garlic
1 carrot, chopped
600 ml MAGGI All Natural Vegetable Liquid Stock
375 g vegetarian hotdogs (optional), sliced
freshly ground black pepper, to taste
bread rolls

Place the split peas in a large saucepan and cover with plenty of cold water. Bring to the boil and simmer for about 40 minutes, until tender. Drain in a colander and set aside. Spray a large saucepan with oil. Add onion, garlic and carrot to the saucepan and cook over medium heat for 5 minutes, stirring occasionally. Stir through the cooked split peas and vegetable stock, and season with pepper. Bring to the boil, then reduce heat to low. Simmer, partially covered, for 15 minutes, adding a little water, if necessary. Add the sliced hotdogs, if using and simmer over medium heat for 5 minutes. Garnish with chervil, if desired. Serve with a crusty bread roll.

ANALYSIS (inc. bread)	4	6
Energy (kJ Cal)	2414 578	1609 384
■ Carb (g)	77	51
■ Prot (g)	39	26
■ Fat (g)	12	8
■ Fibre, Iron, Zinc		

Preparation time: 10 minutes
Cooking time: 1 hour 5 minutes

split-pea chowder

SARAH RYAN ~ swimming
sarah's asian salmon salad
Greatest sporting achievement:
Making the Olympic final in the
100m freestyle event in 1996
and my Olympic silver medal.
Favourite foods:
Omelettes, veal marsala.
My contribution to Survival 2:
I like cooking meals to eat with
my fiancé Gus. We like quick
and easy salads, and who can
resist a nice piece of salmon?

sarah's asian salmon salad Serves 4-6

500 g dried rice vermicelli noodles
1 bunch baby bok choy
150 g snow peas, trimmed
1 large carrot, cut into thin strips
olive or canola oil spray
4 small salmon fillets
1 red capsicum, cut into thin strips
400 g can baby corn, drained and halved lengthways
¼ cup lemon juice
2 tablespoons MAGGI Authentic Thai Sweet Chilli Sauce
1 teaspoon minced ginger

Place noodles in a large heatproof bowl and cover with boiling water. Stand for 10 minutes, then drain and rinse thoroughly with cold water; drain well. Remove the stem ends of the bok choy and separate the leaves. Wash and dry, then cut the leaves from the stems. Cut stems crossways into 1-cm slices, and cut leaves crossways into 2-cm shreds. Put stems, snow peas and carrot in a heatproof bowl and cover with boiling water. Stand for 3 minutes, then drain well. Spray a large nonstick chargrill pan or frying pan with oil and heat. Cook salmon over medium-low heat for 3 minutes on each side. Transfer to a plate, cover loosely with foil and stand for 5 minutes. Meanwhile, place noodles and vegetables in a large bowl. In a small bowl or jug, mix lemon juice, sweet chilli sauce and ginger. Pour over noodle salad and toss well to combine. Divide salad among serving plates, and top with salmon fillet. Season with freshly ground pepper. Garnish with coriander leaves, if desired. Note: If serving six, add another 2 salmon fillets.

ANALYSIS	4	6
Energy (kJ Cal)	1862 445	1241 297
■ Carb (g)	52	34
■ Prot (g)	32	21
■ Fat (g)	11	8
■ Iron, Vitamin C		
■ Zinc		

HINT: *Fresh salmon fillets are delicious but can be expensive. Replace them with two 210 g cans red salmon, drained and flaked into large chunks with a fork. This salad is also delicious with hokkien noodles.*

Preparation time: 20 minutes
Cooking time: 6 minutes

sarah's asian salmon salad

grains

grains

Grains come in a wide variety of forms, flavours and textures and are an extremely versatile way to add carbohydrate to meals. Most can be prepared in minutes and, as an accompaniment or meal base, there are many benefits of grains in an athlete's diet.

Rice / Gone are the days when white rice was the only common variety. These days, you'll easily find short, medium or long grain, brown, wild, basmati, arborio and jasmine as well as various blends of these. All cooked rice offers a whopping 55 grams of carbohydrate per cup. The use of rice is unlimited, so try various types or combinations, and experiment with cooking and flavouring methods. With rice in the cupboard, you'll never go hungry.

Cooking Rice / Cooking times vary according to the type of rice. Brown and wild rice tend to take twice as long as others. Most packs of rice have their own cooking directions, but the commonly used methods include absorption, rapid boil and microwave (see Hints & Tips for cooking instructions).

Polenta / Ground corn with a great colour and unique texture, polenta is usually made into a 'mash' or baked in a slab, then grilled to add flavour or texture. It can also be added to cakes and muffins. One cup of cooked polenta provides 44 grams of carbohydrate.

Risoni / Tiny bits of pasta that look like grains of rice, risoni can be used to thicken soups or casseroles, or in a similar manner to rice. It provides 43 grams of carbohydrate per cup when cooked.

Couscous / Made from semolina (the milled inner wheat grain), couscous readily absorbs flavours. Most available types are 'instant', prepared by covering the couscous with boiling water (mixed with stock or juice for flavour, if preferred). Allow to stand for 5 minutes, or until the water is absorbed. Fluff up couscous using a fork before serving. Couscous is an ideal instant accompaniment. One cup of cooked couscous provides 54 grams of carbohydrate.

Burghul / Made from cracked wheat, burghul adds texture to dishes when combined with other grains such as rice. It's great for salads, especially tabbouli. To prepare, cover burghul in boiling water, soak for 15 minutes, then squeeze out excess water before using. One cup of prepared burghul provides 45 grams of carbohydrate.

hints & tips

➤ To cook rice by absorption: bring 1 cup rice and $1\frac{1}{2}$ cups water to the boil in a saucepan for 1 minute. Cover with a tight-fitting lid, then reduce the heat as low as possible and cook for 10 minutes. Turn off heat, cover and stand for 10 minutes. Fluff up rice using a fork before serving. This method is best for rice eaten with curries and stirfries.

➤ To rapid boil rice: in a large saucepan, bring 2 litres water to the boil and add 1 cup rice. Boil uncovered, 12-15 minutes for white rice and 25-30 minutes for brown or wild rice. Remove a few grains, cool, and taste to check if cooked. When ready, drain rice in a colander and serve. This method is best for fried rice (see below) and rice used in bakes.

➤ To microwave rice: place 1 cup rice and $1\frac{1}{2}$ cups water in a microwave rice-cooker. Cook on HIGH for 5 minutes, then MEDIUM for 10 minutes. Stand, covered, for 5 minutes. Fluff up using a fork before serving. This method produces rice similar to absorption.

➤ Freeze cooked rice for up to 2 months, in meal-size portions in freezer bags or plastic containers. Frozen rice can be reheated in the microwave or by pouring boiling water over it.

➤ Arborio rice is an Italian rice essential for risotto. It can't be substituted with other rice.

➤ Basmati rice is perfect for curries and Indian dishes, while jasmine rice is ideal for stirfries and Thai dishes. Both these rices have subtle fragrances that enhance meals.

➤ Brown rice is long- or medium-grain rice with the outer husk removed and no further processing. It has more fibre than white rice, but it does take longer to cook.

➤ Flavour rice using stock in place of water or add herbs during cooking. Chicken stock, a handful of chopped parsley and $\frac{1}{2}$ teaspoon turmeric goes well in rice served with curry.

➤ Most grains work in sweet dishes, too. Creamed rice is made using the absorption method, replacing water with milk. Sugar, maple syrup, honey or fruit can be added once the rice is cooked. Cooked rice mixed with yogurt or custard makes an extra-quick rice pudding. Or, hydrate couscous with fruit juice and toss in some mixed berries.

➤ Fried rice is best made with rice rapid-boiled the day before as this ensures it won't be gluggy. Place the cooked rice in a covered bowl in the fridge overnight, or, if you're short on time, on a flat tray in the fridge until cooled.

sam's polenta stack

SAM NELSON ~ cycling

sam's polenta stack

Greatest sporting moment:
A-grade rider known for his dedication to the 6 am training bunch during Canberra winters.

Favourite food: Anything fresh with nice bright colours.

My contribution to Survival 2:
As a test subject for the AIS nutrition department's dietary studies, I've given blood, sweat and tears. This polenta stack is one of my favourite recipes (also great with tofu). I hope it saves other athletes from the extreme diets that I've being subjected to during these nutritional tests! So eat up and enjoy.

sam's polenta stack Serves 4-6

Topping:
2 tablespoons orange juice
2 tablespoons honey
2 tablespoons soy sauce
300 g skinless chicken breast fillets
olive or canola oil spray

Polenta base:
300 g can creamed corn
1/2 cup low-fat milk
2 egg whites, lightly beaten
1 cup polenta (cornmeal)
2 teaspoons baking powder
1 large onion, chopped
1/2 cup grated, low-fat cheese

Salsa:
4 medium tomatoes, chopped
1 large mango, chopped
300 g can corn kernels, drained
1 red onion, chopped
2 tablespoons coarsely chopped fresh coriander leaves
1 tablespoon coarsely chopped fresh mint leaves

Preheat oven to 180° (350°F). To make topping, combine juice, honey and soy sauce. Add chicken, stir to coat, and refrigerate for 30 minutes. Spray a chargrill pan or frying pan with oil and heat. Cook chicken for 5–6 minutes on each side until golden brown and tender. Cut into thin slices. To make polenta base, whisk corn, milk and egg whites in a bowl. Stir in polenta and baking powder, then onion and 3/4 of the cheese. Spray a 20 x 30 cm baking tray with oil and pour in mixture. Sprinkle with the remaining cheese. Bake for 30–35 minutes or until golden and firm. To make salsa, mix all ingredients in a bowl until combined. Cut polenta into pieces and serve with chicken slices and salsa.

ANALYSIS	4	6
Energy (kJ Cal)	2251 539	1501 359
■ Carb (g)	77	51
■ Prot (g)	34	22
■ Fat (g)	10	7
■ Vitamin C, Zinc		
■ Calcium, Iron		

Preparation time: 30 minutes + marinating
Cooking time: 50 minutes

mixed mushroom risotto Serves 4-6 ✳

olive or canola oil spray
1 leek, halved lengthways, sliced
500 g mixed mushrooms (e.g. button, swiss, shiitake), sliced
2 cups arborio rice
1½ litres MAGGI All Natural Chicken or Vegetable Liquid Stock
100 g enoki mushrooms
1/4 cup grated fresh Parmesan cheese
2 spring onions, thinly sliced on diagonal

Spray a large saucepan with oil and heat. Add leek and all mushrooms except enoki and cook, stirring, over medium heat for 5 minutes, until softened. Add rice and cook, stirring, for 2 minutes. Add stock, reduce heat and simmer uncovered for 20–25 minutes or until liquid is almost all absorbed. Add enoki mushrooms and cheese and stir well to combine—it should look slightly creamy. Garnish with spring onion and serve with steamed greens or salad. Season to taste.

ANALYSIS	4	6
Energy (kJ Cal)	1960 468	1307 312
■ Carb (g)	87	58
■ Prot (g)	19	12
■ Fat (g)	5	3

HINT: *There is no need to wash or peel the mushrooms—wipe clean using damp paper towels.*

Preparation time: 10 minutes
Cooking time: 35 minutes

mixed mushroom risotto

salmon bake

chicken, corn & chive risotto

salmon bake Serves 4-6 ❄

White sauce:
2 cups low-fat milk
2 tablespoons cornflour
black pepper, to taste

415 g can salmon in water, drained
4 cups cooked brown rice
450 g can pineapple pieces in natural juice, drained
300 g can corn kernels
1 cup chopped red and green capsicum
2 shallots, chopped
black pepper, to taste
1 cup dry breadcrumbs
¼ cup grated low-fat tasty cheese

To make white sauce: pour all but 2 tablespoons milk into a covered microwave dish and cook on HIGH for 2 minutes or until boiling. Mix cornflour with remaining milk until smooth. Add cornflour mixture to hot milk and whisk until well combined. If the sauce is not yet thickening, place in microwave for a further 2 minutes and stir every 30 seconds. Season with black pepper. To make the filling, combine salmon, rice, pineapple, corn, capsicum, shallots and black pepper. Pour into a 30-cm ovenproof dish. Pour white sauce over it and sprinkle combined breadcrumbs and cheese on top. Bake in a preheated 180° (350°F) oven until top is golden brown and salmon is heated through. Serve with a tossed salad. Garnish with chopped chives, if desired.

ANALYSIS		4	6
Energy (kJ Cal)	3308	790	2205 527
▪ Carb (g)		117	78
▪ Prot (g)		47	31
▪ Fat (g)		15	10
▪ Calcium, Iron, Vitamin C, Zinc			

HINT: *This recipe freezes well. Canned tuna or crab can be used instead of salmon.*

Preparation time: 10 minutes
Cooking time: 15 minutes

chicken, corn & chive risotto Serves 4-6 ❄

olive or canola oil spray
1 leek, thinly sliced
400 g chicken breast fillet, cut into thin slices
2 cups arborio rice
1 cup fresh or frozen corn kernels
5 cups MAGGI All Natural Chicken or Vegetable Liquid Stock
1 cup CARNATION Light and Creamy Evaporated Milk
2 teaspoons grated lemon rind
300 g broccoli florets
3 tablespoons snipped fresh chives
pepper and salt, for seasoning

Spray a large pan with oil and heat. Add leek and cook over medium heat for 2–3 minutes or until soft, adding a little water if it starts to stick to the pan. Add chicken and cook, stirring until it starts to brown. Stir through rice and corn and cook for 1 minute. Add the stock, evaporated milk and lemon rind and simmer, uncovered, for 20–25 minutes or until the rice is tender and the liquid has been absorbed, stirring occasionally. Stir in broccoli and chives and season with pepper and salt to taste. Cook, covered, for 5 minutes or until the broccoli is tender but still crisp. Garnish with lemon zest, if desired.

ANALYSIS		4	6
Energy (kJ Cal)	2699	645	1800 430
▪ Carb (g)		99	66
▪ Prot (g)		42	28
▪ Fat (g)		9	6
▪ Iron, Vitamin C, Zinc			
▪ Calcium			

HINT: *Leftover risotto can be shaped into patties and cooked in a lightly oiled pan until crisp and golden and heated through.*

Preparation time: 10 minutes
Cooking time: 40 minutes

RENAE MAYCOCK ~ volleyball
Nestlé sports fellow
chicken, corn & chive risotto
Greatest sporting moment:
Walking into the stadium for the Opening Ceremony of the 2000 Olympics in Sydney.
Favourite part about Survival 1:
The pancakes—I can't believe what a difference the buttermilk makes.
My contribution to Survival 2:
I'm studying nutrition at university, working parttime and training fulltime so I need quick and easy, nutritious foods that taste good. The risotto recipe is great because you just put everything in a pot and stir.

Jambalaya

jambalaya Serves 4-6 ❄

olive or canola oil spray
500 g chicken breast fillet, cut into thin strips
1 large onion, chopped
2 stalks celery, sliced
1 red capsicum, sliced
1 green capsicum, sliced
150 g reduced-fat ham, cut into thin strips
2 cups long-grain rice
400 g can chopped tomatoes
750 ml MAGGI All Natural Chicken or Vegetable Liquid Stock
1/4 cup water
1/2 teaspoon dried thyme
300 g medium green prawns, peeled and deveined, tails left intact
1 cup chopped broccoli
3 tablespoons chopped fresh parsley

Spray a large saucepan with oil and heat. Cook chicken in 2 or 3 batches over high heat for 5 minutes or until browned and tender. Remove from the pan and set aside. Add onion and celery to the pan and cook until they start to soften. Add capsicum and ham and cook for 3 minutes. Add rice and stir until combined. Add tomato, stock, water and thyme and cook, covered, over low heat for 25–30 minutes or until the rice is tender. Stir through the chicken, prawns and broccoli and cook, uncovered, for 5 minutes, stirring occasionally or until the prawns are tender. Serve immediately. Garnish with chopped parsley leaves, if desired.

ANALYSIS	4		6	
Energy (kJ Cal)	2977	711	1985	474
▪ Carb (g)		90		60
▪ Prot (g)		61		41
▪ Fat (g)		12		8
▪ Iron, Vitamin C, Zinc				

HINT: *The chicken breast fillets can be replaced with pork fillets.*

Preparation time: 15 minutes
Cooking time: 55 minutes

japanese beef & vegetables on rice Serves 4-6 ❄

2 cups MAGGI All Natural Chicken or Beef Liquid Stock
1/3 cup reduced-salt soy sauce
3 tablespoons mirin (Japanese sweet rice wine)
2 tablespoons sugar
500 g rump steak, thinly sliced across grain
4 spring onions, sliced
300 g broccoli, cut into florets
200 g snow peas
1 cup fresh or frozen peas
1 red capsicum, sliced
3 eggs, lightly beaten
6 cups cooked Japanese rice or soba noodles
extra spring onions, to garnish

Place stock, soy, mirin and sugar in a large deep saucepan and bring to the boil, reduce heat and simmer for 5 minutes. Add beef and simmer, uncovered, for 5 minutes. Add vegetables and simmer for 3 minutes or until tender. Pour in the eggs in a thin steady stream and allow to spread in the pan; do not stir. Cover and cook over medium heat for 5 minutes until the egg is set. Serve rice in bowls topped with the beef mixture and sprinkled with extra spring onion.

ANALYSIS	4		6	
Energy (kJ Cal)	2847	680	1898	453
▪ Carb (g)		90		60
▪ Prot (g)		50		33
▪ Fat (g)		11		8
▪ Iron, Vitamin C, Zinc				

HINT: *This recipe is also delicious using pork, chicken or lamb. Vegetarians can opt for just vegetables or use sliced, firm tofu.*

Preparation time: 20 minutes
Cooking time: 25 minutes

DEB KERR ~ dietitian
Australian Women's Hockey Team
jambalaya
Favourite part about Survival 1:
I work with the Australian Women's Hockey Team and each time the girls get together, talk centres around recipes they've cooked from Survival 1.
My contribution to Survival 2:
One-pot meals are a favourite with the hockey girls, especially when quick, tasty and packed with nutrients. Jambalaya is sure to be a regular on the team menu.

japanese beef & vegetables on rice

tuna, potato & herb risoni

fried rice

tuna, potato & herb risoni   Serves 4-6   ❋

500 g risoni
2 potatoes (300 g), peeled and cut into 2-cm cubes
250 g sweet potato, peeled and cut into 2-cm cubes
olive or canola oil spray
1 onion, finely chopped
300 g jar tomato and basil pasta sauce
1 tablespoon balsamic vinegar
1 teaspoon sugar
100 g baby spinach leaves
400 g can chunk-style tuna in brine, drained
freshly ground black pepper
2 tablespoons shaved Parmesan cheese

Cook the risoni, potato and sweet potato in a large saucepan of boiling water for 10–12 minutes or until tender. Meanwhile, spray a nonstick frying pan with oil and heat. Add onion and cook over medium heat for 2–3 minutes or until soft. Add pasta sauce, vinegar and sugar. Bring to boil, reduce heat and simmer for 10 minutes or until thickened slightly. Drain risoni and vegetables and return to the saucepan. Add spinach, tuna and pasta sauce mixture, and cook over low heat until heated through. Season with ground black pepper and serve topped with Parmesan. Garnish with coriander leaves, if desired.

ANALYSIS	4	6
Energy (kJ Cal)	2873 686	1915 458
▪ Carb (g)	114	76
▪ Prot (g)	42	28
▪ Fat (g)	6	4
▪ Iron, Vitamin C, Zinc		

HINT: *Risoni is small rice-shaped pasta, available in the dried-pasta section of supermarkets.*

Preparation time: 15 minutes
Cooking time: 20 minutes

fried rice   Serves 4-6   ❋

olive or canola oil spray
2 eggs, lightly beaten
3 spring onions, sliced
1 carrot, thinly sliced
1 red capsicum, sliced
150 g fresh baby corn
1 cup button mushrooms, halved
150 g shaved reduced-fat ham, chopped
6 cups cold cooked rice
1 cup frozen peas
3 tablespoons soy sauce
2 tablespoons MAGGI Authentic Thai Sweet Chilli Sauce

Spray a nonstick wok with oil and heat. Pour in the egg and swirl the pan so that the egg evenly covers the base and side. Cook over medium heat until set. Roll up in the wok, remove, thinly slice and set aside. Lightly spray the wok again with oil and add the spring onion. Stirfry over medium heat for 1 minute or until soft and golden. Add the vegetables and stirfry for 3 minutes until tender. Stir in ham, rice and peas, and cook for 3–4 minutes until the rice is heated through. Stir in shredded egg and soy and sweet chilli sauce until well combined. Garnish with sliced spring onion, if desired. Note: You need 2¼ cups uncooked rice to yield 6 cups cooked rice.

SARAH BARRETT ~ netball
fried rice
Greatest sporting moment:
Winning the World Youth Cup in 2000.
Favourite food: Bananas.
My contribution to Survival 2:
The advantage of making fried rice is that you can add anything from the fridge. I've used my favourite ingredients, but don't feel tied down to the recipe if you want to be adventurous.

ANALYSIS	4	6
Energy (kJ Cal)	2102 502	1402 335
▪ Carb (g)	87	58
▪ Prot (g)	22	15
▪ Fat (g)	7	5
▪ Iron, Vitamin C, Zinc		

HINT: *This recipe makes a great lunch idea. Reheat in a microwave-safe container.*

Preparation time: 10 minutes
Cooking time: 10 minutes

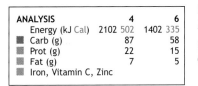

pasta

pasta

These days, pasta is one of the most frequently eaten meals in Australian homes, and it's also a favourite in the AIS Dining Hall. Athletes love pasta—they can utilise its high carbohydrate level and combine it with an endless variety of sauces. But athletes have to be careful, too, and avoid high-fat pasta traps.

In Italian 'pasta' means 'dough', of which there are two main types—dry and fresh. Best made from durum wheat (this may be ground to semolina), pasta comes in an awesome variety of shapes and sizes, some with names that reflect their origins in Italy.

Dry pasta has a very long shelf life, is easy to store and has a low risk of spoiling in the cupboard. Dry pasta is easy and quick to cook—just use a big saucepan which holds about 2 litres of water for each serve of pasta (for example, if cooking pasta for two people you need 4 litres of water). Make sure the water is rapidly boiling before adding the pasta and stir to prevent it from sticking together or to the bottom of the saucepan. Many chefs advocate adding salt and oil to the cooking water, but you can still cook your pasta to perfection without these additions.

Dry pasta takes about 5–12 minutes to become 'al dente'—cooked so that it's still firm but has lost its hard starchy centre. Drain the pasta well but don't rinse it—rinsing removes starch which helps to hold the sauce and is also a rich source of carbohydrate. Resist the temptation to mix oil through the pasta to prevent sticking—it undermines the nutritional goals of many high-carbohydrate meals. If you cook the pasta just before serving, then stir the sauce through, it shouldn't stick together.

Fresh pasta is traditionally made with eggs, but there are also varieties without eggs or with ingredients such as spinach or tomato. You can also buy fresh pasta flavoured with mushroom, saffron, garlic, basil and even chocolate! Its great advantage, apart from flavour, is that fresh pasta cooks very quickly. Use the same method as for dry pasta, making sure the water is rapidly boiling before adding the pasta, and cook for only 2–3 minutes or according to packet instructions.

hints & tips

➤ Pasta is a rich source of carbohydrate: 1 cup (150 g) cooked or fresh pasta or $1/3$ cup (50 g) dry pasta = 37 g carbohydrates.

➤ Matching pasta with sauce is a personal preference, but in general, the thick chunky sauces go best with pasta shapes or tubes such as farfalle (bows) or rigatoni, while creamy or simple sauces suit the long strands of spaghetti or fettucine.

➤ Fresh pasta and leftover cooked pasta will keep for 3–4 days in the refrigerator. Cooked pasta should be placed in the fridge within an hour of cooking and should not be allowed to sit at room temperature for longer periods. Remember to label and date all leftovers and store them in airtight or sealed containers.

➤ Pasta and noodles can be reheated by placing a serving into a wire basket or strainer and plunging into boiling water for a minute. Drain well, and the pasta is ready to serve or mix with sauce. (Alternatively, reheat it briefly in the microwave.)

➤ Our lasagne recipes use more pasta and less filling to ensure a high-carbohydrate, low-fat content. To do this, simply use thin layers of filling and put a sheet of pasta in between each different layer in the dish—you should be able to double the number of pasta sheets used in regular lasagnes.

➤ Creamy pasta sauces can be high-fat traps for athletes, but you can easily convert your favourite into a low-fat alternative. Simply substitute evaporated skim milk thickened with cornflour for the cream or milk in the sauce (mix 1–2 teaspoons of cornflour with every 375 ml of evaporated milk).

➤ Cheese is another high-fat ingredient which quickly unbalances the fat and carbohydrate content of a pasta dish. Reduced-fat cheeses are still high-fat foods so use them sparingly. Try using strongly flavoured cheese such as Parmesan so that you only need a small amount to get the desired effect.

➤ Other high-fat traps to watch out for are filled pastas like tortellini and ravioli—some of the fillings are very high in fat.

pumpkin pasta for kate   Serves 4-6 ❅

500 g pasta spirals
2 kg butternut pumpkin, peeled and cut into 2-cm cubes
50 g pine nuts
olive or canola oil spray
1 onion, finely chopped
375 ml can CARNATION Light and Creamy Evaporated Milk
black pepper, to taste
pinch of ground nutmeg
1 small green capsicum and 1 small red capsicum, cut into long thin strips
100 g cherry tomatoes, halved
1 carrot, cut into thin strips
½ teaspoon minced ginger
½ teaspoon finely chopped fresh red chilli

Cook pasta according to packet instructions. Meanwhile, steam or microwave pumpkin until tender. Heat a large nonstick frying pan over medium heat. Cook pine nuts for 1 minute, stirring frequently, or until lightly golden. Set aside. Spray a medium saucepan with oil and heat. Cook onion over medium heat for 2–3 minutes until soft and lightly golden. Add pumpkin, mash until pumpkin is smooth, gradually adding milk. Season with black pepper and nutmeg. Slowly bring to boil over medium heat. Spray a frying pan with oil and heat. Stirfry capsicum, tomato, carrot, ginger and chilli over medium-high heat for 3 minutes, until tender-crisp. Drain pasta and divide among serving bowls, then ladle sauce over. Top with vegetables and pine nuts. Garnish with chives, if desired.

ANALYSIS	4	6
Energy (kJ Cal)	3289 786	2193 524
▪ Carb (g)	129	86
▪ Prot (g)	34	22
▪ Fat (g)	15	10
▪ Calcium, Fibre, Vitamin C, Zinc		
▪ Iron		

Preparation time: 20 minutes
Cooking time: 15 minutes

spinach fettucine with eggplant & chickpeas

Serves 4-6 ❅

olive or canola oil spray
1 onion, chopped
2 teaspoons minced garlic
4 slender eggplants, thickly sliced
3 large zucchini, halved lengthways and thickly sliced
825 g can crushed tomatoes
375 ml MAGGI All Natural Vegetable Liquid Stock
400 g can chickpeas, rinsed and drained
1 teaspoon dried Italian herbs
2 teaspoons sugar
500 g spinach fettucine
400 g can artichoke hearts, drained and quartered
ground black pepper, to taste

Spray a large saucepan with oil and heat. Add onion and cook over medium heat for 3 minutes or until soft. Add garlic and cook for 1 minute more. Add eggplant, zucchini, tomato, stock, chickpeas, herbs and sugar. Bring to the boil, reduce heat and simmer, partially covered, for 10 minutes. Uncover and cook a further 10 minutes, stirring regularly, until vegetables are tender and sauce has thickened slightly. Meanwhile, cook spinach pasta according to packet directions. Stir artichokes into the sauce and heat through. Season with black pepper. Drain pasta and serve with sauce. Garnish with chervil, if desired.

HINT: *Keep this sauce in the fridge for up to 3 days or freeze for up to 3 months.*

ANALYSIS	4	6
Energy (kJ Cal)	2622 626	1748 418
▪ Carb (g)	115	77
▪ Prot (g)	27	18
▪ Fat (g)	6	4
▪ Fibre, Vitamin C		
▪ Iron		

Preparation time: 15 minutes
Cooking time: 25 minutes

pumpkin pasta for kate

KATE SMITH ~ basketball
pumpkin pasta for kate
Greatest sporting achievement:
Being on the Australian Gem squad (National Under-20 basketball team).
Favourite food: Breakfast cereal.
Contribution to Survival 2:
I recently decided to adopt a vegetarian eating style. At one of our cooking classes, the other basketball girls decided to create a recipe especially for me—pumpkin and vegetable sauce for pasta. It's now a masterpiece!

spinach fettucine with eggplant & chickpeas

spaghetti with chilli beef & beans

fettucine with moroccan-style lamb sauce

spaghetti with chilli beef & beans   Serves 4-6 ❋

olive or canola oil spray

500 g lean beef mince

2 teaspoons Mexican chilli powder

250 ml MAGGI All Natural Beef Liquid Stock

575 g jar tomato-based pasta sauce

440 g can red kidney beans, rinsed and drained

300 g can corn kernels, drained

1 green capsicum, diced

500 g spaghetti

Spray a large saucepan with oil and heat. Add beef and chilli powder and cook over medium heat for about 5 minutes, until browned, breaking up any lumps. Stir in stock and pasta sauce, and bring to the boil. Reduce heat and simmer, partially covered, for 15 minutes, stirring occasionally. Add beans and vegetables and cook a further 5 minutes. While sauce is simmering, cook pasta in a large saucepan of boiling water. Drain and serve with the sauce. Garnish with shredded parsley and spring onions, if desired. Note: Mexican chilli powder, a blend of herbs and ground chilli is not as hot as regular chilli powder, so if substituting with chilli powder, use half the amount.

HINT: *This sauce keeps in the fridge for up to 2 days—in fact, the flavour improves if made ahead. It can also be frozen for up to 2 months. Freeze individual portions (remember to label and date them), and when required, transfer to the fridge in the morning for eating that night.*

ANALYSIS	4	6
Energy (kJ Cal)	3574 854	2383 569
▪ Carb (g)	130	86
▪ Prot (g)	52	35
▪ Fat (g)	13	9
▪ Fibre, Iron, Zinc		

Preparation time: 10 minutes
Cooking time: 25 minutes

fettucine with moroccan-style lamb sauce

Serves 4-6 ❋

olive or canola oil spray

1 onion, chopped

3 stalks celery, chopped

2 teaspoons minced garlic

3 teaspoons ground coriander

3 teaspoons ground cumin

500 g lamb mince

250 ml MAGGI All Natural Chicken Liquid Stock

400 g can crushed tomatoes

500 g sweet potato, peeled, cut into 2-cm cubes

2 zucchini, halved lengthways and thickly sliced

500 g fettucine

DAMIEN BURROUGHS ~ athletics
spaghetti with chilli beef & beans
Greatest sporting moment:
Gold Medal in discus at the 1996 Paralympic Games, Atlanta.
Favourite food: Kiwifruit.
My contribution to Survival 2:
I like to think that this book was developed for me as I was continually bugging the nutrition team at the AIS for new recipes. I swear I've cooked every dish in Survival 1— I'm ready for a new challenge.

Spray a large saucepan with oil and heat. Cook onion and celery for 3–4 minutes, or until soft. Add garlic and spices and cook for 1 minute more. Add lamb and cook, stirring, for 5 minutes over high heat, or until browned, breaking up any lumps with back of wooden spoon. Add stock, tomato and sweet potato. Bring to the boil, reduce heat and simmer, partially covered, for 10 minutes. Add zucchini and cook, uncovered, over medium heat for 15 minutes, stirring regularly, until vegetables are tender and sauce has thickened. While sauce is simmering, cook pasta in a large saucepan of boiling water according to packet instructions. Drain and serve topped with sauce. Garnish with sliced spring onions, and chopped parsley, if desired.

ANALYSIS	4	6
Energy (kJ Cal)	3039 726	2026 484
▪ Carb (g)	110	73
▪ Prot (g)	45	30
▪ Fat (g)	11	8
▪ Iron, Vitamin C, Zinc		

HINT: *This sauce will keep in the fridge for up to 2 days—in fact, the flavour improves if made ahead. It can also be frozen for up to 2 months, in individual portions for convenience, if desired.*

Preparation time: 10 minutes
Cooking time: 35 minutes

spirals with lamb, feta & vegetables Serves 4-6 ❄

500 g spiral pasta
2 corn cobs
olive or canola oil spray
400 g trim lamb fillets
1 red onion, cut into thin wedges
1 green capsicum, cut into thin strips
2 zucchini, thinly sliced
150 g button mushrooms, sliced
1 punnet cherry tomatoes, halved
60 g fetta cheese, crumbled

Cook pasta according to packet instructions. Husk corn and remove silk. Stand cobs on an angle on a board and use a small sharp knife in a downward motion to cut off the kernels. Spray a large nonstick frying pan or wok with oil and heat. Cook half the lamb for 2–3 minutes until browned and cooked through. Repeat with remaining lamb. Transfer to a plate, cover loosely with foil, and stand for 5 minutes. Thinly slice across grain and set aside. Reheat frying pan (spray again, if needed) and cook corn, onion, capsicum, zucchini and mushroom for 3 minutes. Add tomato, stirfry for another 2 minutes. When cooked, drain pasta and return to the saucepan. Add vegetables and lamb, and stir to combine. Serve topped with crumbled fetta cheese. Garnish with parsley and sliced spring onions, if desired.

ANALYSIS	4	6
Energy (kJ Cal)	2826 675	1884 450
Carb (g)	104	69
Prot (g)	44	29
Fat (g)	9	6
Iron, Vitamin C, Zinc		

HINT: *This recipe is best served immediately. Vary with chicken, and add chopped black olives.*

Preparation time: 15 minutes
Cooking time: about 10 minutes

spirals with lamb, fetta & vegetables

DEBBIE WATSON ~ water polo
spirals with lamb, fetta & vegetables

Greatest sporting moment:
Gold Medal at 2000 Olympic Games in Sydney.

Favourite food: I finish every main meal with ice cream.

My contribution to Survival 2:
This recipe includes one of my favourite foods—fetta cheese. Most people only eat fetta in salads and believe me, they're missing out. Fetta is great used in recipes and adds a taste sensation of its own.

farfalle with chicken & sundried-tomato pesto Serves 4-6 ❄

500 g farfalle pasta (bows)
100 g dried sundried tomatoes, soaked in hot water for 10 minutes, then drained
2 teaspoons minced garlic
1 tablespoon toasted pine nuts
2 tablespoons finely grated Parmesan cheese
2 teaspoons olive oil, plus olive or canola oil spray
⅓ cup MAGGI All Natural Chicken or Vegetable Liquid Stock
500 g chicken breast fillets, thinly sliced
1 red capsicum, sliced lengthways
100 g button mushrooms, quartered
80 g baby English spinach leaves
ground black pepper, to taste

Cook pasta according to packet instructions. Place tomatoes, garlic, pine nuts and cheese in a food processor and process until finely chopped. With motor running, gradually add oil and stock. Process until well combined. Spray a nonstick frying pan with oil and heat. Cook chicken over medium-high heat for 5 minutes or until browned and cooked through. Transfer to a plate, cover loosely with foil and set aside. In the frying pan, stirfry capsicum for 1 minute, then add mushrooms and cook for a further 2 minutes until just soft. Drain cooked pasta and return to the saucepan. Add tomato mixture, stir to coat, then add chicken and vegetables and toss to combine. Season with black pepper and serve with bread. Note: Use dry sundried tomatoes rather than those which are pre-soaked in oil.

ANALYSIS	4	6
Energy (kJ Cal)	3043 727	2028 485
Carb (g)	96	64
Prot (g)	47	32
Fat (g)	16	11
Iron, Vitamin C, Zinc		

HINT: *This recipe can also be eaten as pasta salad. Keep in the fridge for up to 24 hours, but remove well before serving so it isn't too chilled.*

Preparation time: 20 minutes
Cooking time: 10 minutes

farfalle with chicken & sundried-tomato pesto

david's salami pasta

vegetable lasagne

david's salami pasta Serves 4-6 ❋

500 g pasta spirals
olive or canola oil spray
1 onion, sliced
2 teaspoons minced garlic
150 g salami slices, chopped
825 g can crushed tomatoes
1 teaspoon dried basil
1 teaspoon dried oregano
125 ml red wine or MAGGI All Natural Beef Liquid Stock
3 tablespoons grated Parmesan cheese

Cook pasta according to packet instructions. Spray a large nonstick frying pan with oil and heat. Cook onion over medium heat for 3 minutes or until soft. Add garlic and cook for 1 minute. Add salami and cook for 2-3 minutes. Add tomato, herbs and wine and bring to boil. Reduce heat to low and simmer for 4-5 minutes. When cooked, drain pasta and place in serving bowls. Top with sauce and sprinkle with cheese. Garnish with chopped chives, if desired.

ANALYSIS		4		6
Energy (kJ Cal)	2686	685	1912	457
▪ Carb (g)		94		63
▪ Prot (g)		26		17
▪ Fat (g)		20		13
▪ Iron, Zinc				

Preparation time: 10 minutes
Cooking time: 15 minutes

vegetable lasagne Serves 4-6 ❋

Lasagne filling:
1 cup Vitaburger (textured vegetable protein)
2 zucchini, diced
1 large carrot, diced
1 onion, diced
1 small green capsicum and 1 small red capsicum, diced
8 mushrooms, diced
575 g jar tomato-based pasta sauce
375 ml MAGGI All Natural Vegetable Liquid Stock
5 tablespoons tomato paste
1 tablespoon tomato sauce
1 tablespoon soy sauce
1 teaspoon minced garlic
1-2 teaspoons dried mixed herbs
black pepper, to taste

Cheese sauce:
375 g low-fat ricotta cheese
375 ml low-fat milk
2 tablespoons grated Parmesan cheese, plus 2 extra tablespoons
1 tablespoon cornflour

olive or canola oil spray
375 g packet fresh lasagne sheets

Preheat oven to 180°C (350°F). In a large bowl, combine all filling ingredients, then set aside. To make cheese sauce, combine ricotta, milk (set aside 1 tablespoon) and 2 tablespoons parmesan in a microwave-safe bowl. Heat on HIGH for 4 minutes. In a small bowl, stir reserved milk and cornflour until smooth. Stir cornflour into cheese mixture and heat for 30 seconds on HIGH. Stir well and set aside. Spray a large lasagne dish with oil. Start layers: first the pasta (trimmed to fit), then the filling. Repeat layers until all sheets are used, finishing with a pasta layer. Pour cheese sauce over the top and sprinkle with the extra cheese. Bake for 1 hour until top is golden brown. Serve with salad and crusty bread. Garnish with chervil, if desired.

ANALYSIS		4		6
Energy (kJ Cal)	2983	713	1989	475
▪ Carb (g)		87		58
▪ Prot (g)		54		36
▪ Fat (g)		16		11
▪ Calcium, Fibre, Iron, Vitamin C, Zinc				

Preparation time: 25 minutes
Cooking time: 1 hour 5 minutes

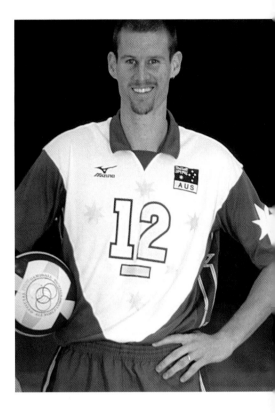

DAVID BEARD ~ volleyball
david's salami pasta
Greatest sporting moment:
Finishing 8th at the 2000
Olympics in Sydney.
Favourite food: Everything—my
teammates can vouch for that!
But it's hard for me to go past
Vita Brits and Weeties.
My contribution to Survival 2:
My salami recipe is one that
I invented while I was playing
in the Italian Volleyball League.
We had to get creative with
pasta because there's not much
else to use over there. So
I thought of some things that
might taste good together,
gave it a whirl, and voila!

penne primavera Serves 4-6 ✳

500 g penne
2 large carrots, halved lengthways and thinly sliced
2 large zucchini, halved lengthways and thinly sliced
200 g broccoli, cut into small florets
125 g snow peas, halved diagonally
1 tablespoon cornflour
375 ml can CARNATION Light and Creamy Evaporated Milk
2 MAGGI Vegetable or Chicken Stock Cubes
1½ tablespoons finely grated Parmesan cheese, optional

Cook the pasta according to packet instructions. Steam or microwave the vegetables until just tender and brightly coloured, taking care not to overcook. Put cornflour in a small bowl and gradually add ⅓ cup evaporated milk, stirring until smooth. Add remaining evaporated milk to a small saucepan, and crumble in the stock cubes. Add cornflour mixture to the saucepan, and stir over medium heat until the mixture boils and thickens. When the pasta is cooked, drain and serve with sauce, topped with the vegetables and a sprinkle of Parmesan cheese. Garnish with chopped flat-leaf parsley, if desired.

ANALYSIS	4		6	
Energy (kJ Cal)	2413	576	1608	384
▪ Carb (g)		104		69
▪ Prot (g)		28		18
▪ Fat (g)		5		3
▪ Calcium, Vitamin C				
▪ Zinc				

HINT: *This recipe is best served immediately. Increase protein by cutting 2 skinless chicken breast fillets into thin strips, then panfry for 5 minutes. Add the chicken to the pasta with the vegetables.*

Preparation time: 15 minutes
Cooking time: 10 minutes

b's penne with butter beans & tuna Serves 4-6 ✳

500 g penne pasta
1 tablespoon olive oil
3 tomatoes, chopped
1 small red onion, cut into thin wedges
425 g can tuna in brine, drained and flaked
2 x 300 g cans butter beans, rinsed and drained
½ cup coarsely chopped continental parsley leaves
2 tablespoons coarsely chopped capers
2 tablespoons lemon juice
ground black pepper, to taste

Cook pasta according to packet instructions. Drain well, then place into a large bowl. Toss the pasta with the olive oil while still warm. Add the remaining ingredients, stir well to combine and season with black pepper. Divide among bowls to serve.

HINT: *This recipe can be served immediately, or as a pasta salad. Keep the salad refrigerated for up to 24 hours, but remove from the fridge well before serving so that it isn't too chilled.*

Preparation time: 15 minutes
Cooking time: 10 minutes

ANALYSIS	4		6	
Energy (kJ Cal)	2689	642	1793	428
▪ Carb (g)		92		62
▪ Prot (g)		45		30
▪ Fat (g)		9		6
▪ Iron, Vitamin C, Zinc				

penne primavera

BENITA WILLIS ~ athletics
Nestlé sports fellow
b's penne with butter beans & tuna
Greatest sporting moment: Running in front of a packed stadium of roaring Aussies during the 2000 Olympics.
Favourite food: Seafood, chocolate milkshakes and apples.
My contribution to Survival 2: Because I love seafood, my tuna pasta is quick and easy to prepare, inexpensive, and ideal for people with busy lifestyles. It's low in fat and nutritious, too, and uses ingredients that you would normally have in the pantry.

B's penne with butter beans & tuna

petria's mexican chicken cannelloni

pasta frittata

petria's mexican chicken cannelloni Serves 4-6 ✳

olive or canola oil spray

500 g lean chicken mince

1 red capsicum, finely chopped

400 g can red kidney beans, drained and rinsed

200 g jar Mexican salsa or taco sauce

575 g jar tomato-based pasta sauce

375 g packet fresh lasagne sheets

420 g can tomato soup

½ cup grated reduced-fat tasty cheese

Preheat oven to 180°C (350°F). Spray a large nonstick frying pan with oil. Add chicken and capsicum, and cook for 5 minutes over high heat, breaking up the mince with back of spoon. Add beans, salsa and pasta sauce, stir until combined and remove from the heat. Cut pasta sheets crossways into thirds and lay out on a board. Spoon a line of filling lengthways along the middle of each piece, and carefully roll to create a tube. Arrange tubes closely together in a large baking dish, joined side down. Pour over tomato soup and sprinkle with grated cheese. Bake for 20–25 minutes until cheese is brown. Serve with salad. Garnish with chervil, if desired. Note: You may need two baking dishes for this recipe.

HINT: *Mexican salsa and taco sauce can be mild, medium or hot—use whichever you prefer.*

Preparation time: 20 minutes
Cooking time: 30 minutes

ANALYSIS		4	6
Energy (kJ Cal)	2902	693	1935 462
▪ Carb (g)		89	59
▪ Prot (g)		46	31
▪ Fat (g)		17	12
▪ Fibre, Iron, Vitamin C, Zinc			
▪ Calcium			

pasta frittata Serves 4-6

250 g spaghetti

150 g sweet potato, cut into small cubes

olive or canola oil spray

1 onion, chopped

2 rashers bacon, chopped

1 red capsicum, cut into small pieces

100 g button mushrooms, halved and sliced

310 g can corn kernels, drained

½ cup fresh flat-leaf parsley, chopped

3 eggs

5 egg whites

Italian crusty bread, to serve

Cook pasta according to packet instructions. Steam or microwave sweet potato until tender. Meanwhile, spray a frying pan with oil and heat. Add onion, bacon and capsicum and cook over medium heat for 4 minutes until vegetables are soft and bacon is brown. Add mushrooms and cook for another minute until soft. Transfer to a large bowl, and add sweet potato, corn, parsley and drained spaghetti; mix well. Spray a nonstick frying pan (30 cm across top) with oil and heat. Arrange spaghetti mixture evenly over base of pan. Whisk eggs and egg whites in a jug until well combined. Pour evenly over spaghetti mixture. Cook over medium heat for about 8 minutes, moving the pan around, if necessary, to cook the frittata evenly. Preheat a grill to medium and place the frying pan under the grill (be careful not to burn wooden or plastic handles) for 6–7 minutes, until set. Carefully run a spatula around the edge of the frittata. Place a large plate face down over the frittata, and carefully invert to turn out. Cut into pieces to serve. Serve with a salad and bread, if desired. Note: The frittata keeps in the fridge for up to 2 days and can be reheated or eaten cold or at room temperature.

Preparation time: 15 minutes
Cooking time: 25 minutes

ANALYSIS (inc. bread)		4	6
Energy (kJ Cal)	2916	697	1944 464
▪ Carb (g)		105	70
▪ Prot (g)		32	21
▪ Fat (g)		16	11
▪ Iron, Vitamin C			
▪ Zinc			

PETRIA THOMAS ~ swimming
petria's mexican chicken cannelloni
Greatest sporting achievement:
Coming back twice from shoulder reconstructions.
Favourite food:
Roast dinner.
Contribution to Survival 2:
I loved the lasagnes in Survival 1. I took the ideas from those lasagne recipes and made a cannelloni variation.

stephan's napolitana sauce   Serves 4-6   ❋

olive or canola oil spray
1 onion, finely chopped
3 cloves garlic, finely chopped
3 tablespoons tomato paste
825 g can crushed tomatoes
250 ml (1 cup) MAGGI All Natural Chicken or Vegetable Liquid Stock
1½ teaspoons dried thyme
1½ teaspoons dried basil
1½ teaspoons dried oregano
2 bay leaves
½ teaspoon ground black pepper
1½ teaspoons caster sugar
500 g penne pasta

Spray a large saucepan with oil and heat. Add onion and garlic and cook over medium-low heat for 2–3 minutes until just soft and transparent. Add tomato paste, and cook, stirring, for 30 seconds. Add crushed tomatoes and stock. Increase heat to medium, cover and bring to the boil. Reduce heat to low, uncover, and stir in herbs, pepper and sugar. Simmer for 30 minutes, stirring occasionally until thickened. Meanwhile, cook pasta according to packet instructions. Drain and serve topped with the sauce. Garnish with chopped fresh chives, if desired.

HINT: *This sauce keeps in the fridge for up to 2 days—in fact, the flavour improves if made ahead. It can also be frozen for up to 2 months. Freeze individual portions and when required, transfer them from the freezer to the fridge in the morning to eat that night.*

ANALYSIS	4	6
Energy (kJ Cal)	2053 438	1368 327
■ Carb (g)	97	65
■ Prot (g)	17	12
■ Fat (g)	3	2
■ Fibre, Vitamin C		
■ Iron		

Preparation time: 15 minutes
Cooking time: 40 minutes

stephan's napolitana sauce

KATE FAIRWEATHER ~ archery
stephan's napolitana sauce
Greatest sporting achievement:
Shooting as part of Australia's most successful Olympic Archery team.
Favourite food: Anything spicy, flavoursome, and vegetarian.
Contribution to Survival 2:
My husband Stephan, a chef, often makes large quantities of 'Nap' sauce and freezes it. It's our 'fall-back' option and so versatile—use it on its own, or as part of other recipes such as in lasagne, over vegetables with polenta, or on a pizza.

creamy seafood sauce   Serves 4-6   ❋

500 g penne pasta
olive or canola oil spray
1 onion, finely chopped
1 tablespoon cornflour
375 ml can CARNATION Light and Creamy Evaporated Milk
2 tablespoons lemon juice
2 teaspoons finely grated lemon rind
500 g seafood marinara mix
2 tablespoons chopped fresh flat-leaf parsley
ground black pepper, to taste

Cook pasta according to packet instructions. Meanwhile, spray a large nonstick deep frying pan with oil and heat. Add onion and cook over medium heat for 2–3 minutes or until soft. Put cornflour in a small bowl and gradually add ⅓ cup milk, stirring until smooth. Add remaining milk to the pan, then gradually add cornflour mixture, stirring constantly. Keep stirring slowly until the mixture boils and thickens. Stir in lemon juice and rind, then add seafood and cook for 4–5 minutes or until cooked through. Stir in parsley and season to taste. When cooked, drain the pasta, divide among bowls and top with sauce. Serve with salad and crusty bread. Garnish with lemon zest and chopped parsley, if desired.

ANALYSIS	4	6
Energy (kJ Cal)	2766 661	1844 441
■ Carb (g)	105	70
■ Prot (g)	45	30
■ Fat (g)	6	4
■ Calcium, Iron, Zinc		

HINT: *This recipe is best served immediately. Serve with a mixed salad for extra nutrients.*

Preparation time: 10 minutes
Cooking time: 10 minutes

creamy seafood sauce

popeye lasagne

pasta bake

popeye lasagne   Serves 4-6   ✳

Meat sauce:
olive or canola oil spray
1 medium onion, finely chopped
2 teaspoons minced garlic
600 g lean beef mince
575 g jar tomato-based pasta sauce
400 g can crushed tomatoes

Spinach and ricotta layer:
250 g packet frozen chopped spinach, thawed
375 g low-fat ricotta cheese

375 g packet fresh lasagne sheets
1/2 cup grated reduced-fat tasty cheese

Preheat oven to 180°C (350°F). To make meat sauce, spray a large nonstick frying pan with oil and heat. Cook onion and garlic over medium heat for 2 minutes, until soft. Add mince and cook over high heat for 5 minutes until brown, using a wooden spoon to break up any lumps. Stir in pasta sauce and tomato, then remove from heat. Drain spinach and squeeze out excess liquid. Place in a bowl and mix with ricotta. Trim pasta sheets to fit a large lasagne dish, and spread a vary thin layer of meat sauce over the base. Arrange a layer of pasta over sauce. Divide remaining sauce and spinach mixture into 3 portions each. Start with a thin layer of sauce, then pasta sheets, then spinach mixture. Continue layering, finishing with the spinach mixture. Sprinkle with tasty cheese. Bake for 30 minutes until heated through and the top is golden brown.

HINT: *To freeze leftover lasagne, place the dish in the fridge until the lasagne is firm and cold, then cut into serving portions. Wrap each portion in foil, then seal in airtight plastic bags or containers. Freeze for up to 2 months. To thaw, place lasagne in the fridge for 24 hours. Reheat on a baking tray for about 30 minutes in a preheated moderate oven.*

ANALYSIS		4	6
Energy (kJ Cal)	3077	735	2051 490
▦ Carb (g)		85	57
▦ Prot (g)		52	35
▦ Fat (g)		20	14
▦ Calcium, Fibre, Iron, Zinc			

Preparation time: 20 minutes
Cooking time: 40 minutes

MICHELLE GILLETT ~ netball
popeye lasagne
Greatest sporting moment:
Winning the World Youth Cup
in 2000.
Favourite food: I really like
pizza, and MILO Bars.
My contribution to Survival 2:
In the past, I've struggled to
eat sufficient iron in my diet.
Now, I'm on an iron-intake
program and always on the
hunt for iron-rich recipes. The
popeye lasagne is not only rich
in iron, it's also a great source
of calcium, protein and
carbohydrate.

pasta bake   Serves 4-6   ✳

500 g macaroni
375 g packet vegetarian sausages, sliced
400 g can crushed tomatoes
3 stalks celery, chopped
1 green capsicum, chopped
2 carrots, grated
250 ml MAGGI All Natural Vegetable Liquid Stock
1 teaspoon dried mixed herbs
1/2 teaspoon minced garlic
1 tablespoon soy sauce
1/2 cup grated low-fat tasty cheese

Preheat oven to 180°C (350°F). Cook macaroni according to packet instructions until al dente. Drain well. Place in a large bowl and add all the other ingredients, except for the cheese. Stir until well combined. Transfer to a 3-litre ovenproof casserole dish. Sprinkle the cheese over the top, and bake for 30–40 minutes or until heated through and the cheese is golden and bubbling. Garnish with chervil, if desired.

ANALYSIS		4	6
Energy (kJ Cal)	2746	656	1830 437
▦ Carb (g)		97	65
▦ Prot (g)		37	24
▦ Fat (g)		12	8
▦ Vitamin C			
▦ Calcium, Iron, Zinc			

Preparation time: 20 minutes
Cooking time: 50 minutes

spice

spice

Today's athletes don't have time for fussy meal preparation which is why curries and stirfries are perfect—one-pot cooking, quick, and packed with taste. And, using basic techniques, there is an infinite variety of dishes that can be created.

The possibilities are endless when choosing ingredients for curries and stirfries—beef, lamb, pork, chicken, seafood, tofu or nuts combined with vegetables and fruit and, of course, the sauces and spices. Accompaniments include rice in all its forms, noodles, pasta, couscous, poppadoms, chappatis, naan bread and many more.

Good preparation is essential for any one-pot meal. Food should be chopped, packets opened and ingredients measured before cooking begins. Meat should be cut evenly to ensure uniform cooking. Cut slower cooking vegetables into small pieces or cook them before other softer vegetables (see Hints & Tips).

A good nonstick wok, frying pan or saucepan is necessary for curries and stirfries, allowing high heat and minimal oil to be used. It is essential to heat the pan before adding any ingredients. Once they're in, the ingredients need to be moved about to ensure even cooking—which is why woks, with their curved sides, are ideal.

For stirfries, cook the meat or tofu first, remove from the pan, and set aside while the vegetables are cooked. Cook meat in small batches to keep the pan hot. Lean meats must be cooked quickly to seal in juices and flavour. Only return the meat or tofu to the pan at the end of cooking to be quickly reheated. This helps keep the meat tender and juicy and prevents the tofu from breaking up.

Accompaniments such as rice and noodles may take longer to prepare than the dish itself, so plan for all parts of the meal to be ready for eating at the same time. Take advantage of the variety of noodles available, as many of these only require a quick soak in boiling water before using. Some, such as fresh hokkien noodles, are high in carbohydrate. Others, such as rice noodles, are lower in carbohydrate so you'll have to consume a larger quantity. For really convenient accompaniments, poppadoms or breads such as pitta, naan and chappatis are great carbohydrate sources.

hints & tips

➤ Choose lean cuts of meat such as beef, rump, fillet or round steak; lamb fillets, eye of loin or butterflies; chicken breast fillets; or butterflied pork steaks, leg steaks or fillets. To simplify matters, look for 'Trim Lamb' and 'New Fashioned Pork'. Meat is most tender when sliced across the grain (lines in the flesh). Marinating helps tenderise meat and adds additional flavour.

➤ Some tofu is available pre-seasoned to add extra flavour. Experiment to find the ones which you think best suit certain dishes.

➤ Onion, cauliflower, broccoli, carrots and potato are the slowest cooking vegetables and should be added first when cooking. Mushrooms, asparagus, zucchini, squash, peas, cabbage and eggplant can be added later. Leafy vegetables such as spinach, bok choy and sprouts should be added at the last minute as they wilt quickly.

➤ Frozen vegetables are great when time is especially limited—they have just as many vitamins and minerals as fresh varieties.

➤ If your stirfry becomes a little dry when cooking, add 1 tablespoon water.

➤ Traditionally, curries can be high in fat due to the use of ghee, oil, coconut cream and butter. But, they can easily be low-fat, too—just reduce the oil and make your own coconut milk by adding 1 teaspoon coconut essence to 1 can CARNATION Light and Creamy Evaporated Milk.

➤ Herbs can really improve the flavour of a curry or stirfry, so try adding basil, coriander, parsley, chives, mint or lemongrass to your favourite dish. Many herbs are available minced and some are already blended in interesting combinations. Fresh herbs are best for a flavour boost, some can be frozen, and they also make great garnishes.

➤ If your curry becomes a little too fiery, add 1 tablespoon low-fat natural yogurt. Combine chopped cucumber, mint and low-fat natural yogurt for a cooling accompaniment. A tomato-based salad is another good choice.

➤ Cook poppadoms in the microwave to keep the fat content low, and briefly warm breads such as pitta, naan and chappati in the oven or microwave.

chilli tofu & noodle stirfry

ED DENIS ~ water polo
chilli tofu & noodle stirfry

Greatest sporting moment: Final qualification game for the medal round against Greece at the World Championships, Perth 1998.

Favourite food: Risotto or my secret pasta dish (this recipe has not yet been revealed!).

My contribution to Survival 2: This stirfry recipe caters to my enjoyment of watching and smelling a meal develop. I like cooking to be a hit on the senses—sight, smell and touch—before it is a hit in the stomach.

chilli tofu & noodle stirfry   Serves 4-6   ❄

900 g fresh hokkien noodles (or udon noodles, if preferred)
olive or canola oil spray
350 g firm tofu, cut into cubes
1 teaspoon minced garlic
1 teaspoon minced ginger
1 onion, sliced into thin wedges
1 small red capsicum, sliced
1 zucchini, sliced
1 carrot, sliced
200 g fresh baby corn
1 bunch broccolini, coarsely chopped
½ cup MAGGI Stir Fry Sauce
3 tablespoons MAGGI Chilli Sauce
2 tablespoons toasted sesame seeds

Place noodles in a large heatproof bowl, cover with boiling water and leave to stand for 2 minutes, gently using a wooden spoon to separate strands. Spray a nonstick wok or frying pan with oil and heat. Cook tofu in 2 or 3 batches over high heat until browned; set aside. Reheat wok, add garlic, ginger, onion and stirfry for 2 minutes or until soft. Add remaining vegetables and stirfry for 3–5 minutes until tender but still crisp. Add drained noodles, tofu and combined sauces to wok. Stirfry for 2 minutes or until heated through. Toss with sesame seeds and serve immediately. Garnish with chervil, if desired.

ANALYSIS		4		6
Energy (kJ Cal)	2368	566	1579	377
◼ Carb (g)		88		58
◼ Prot (g)		26		17
◼ Fat (g)		12		8
◾ Calcium, Fibre, Iron, Vitamin C, Zinc				

Preparation time: 10 minutes
Cooking time: 15 minutes

stirfry fish with lemongrass & asian greens

Serves 4-6

900 g hokkien noodles
olive or canola oil spray
500 g firm fish steaks (e.g. snapper, swordfish, marlin, tuna), cut into large cubes
1 teaspoon minced garlic
1 teaspoon minced ginger
2 stalks lemongrass, finely chopped
1 red onion, sliced
250 g baby bok choy, leaves separated
1 bunch Chinese broccoli, coarsely chopped
1 cup sliced green capsicum
2 tablespoons hoisin sauce
1 tablespoon MAGGI Oyster Sauce
1 tablespoon salt-reduced soy sauce
1 tablespoon rice vinegar
100 g bean sprouts

Place noodles in a large heatproof bowl, cover with boiling water and leave to stand for 2 minutes, gently using a wooden spoon to separate strands. Drain well. Spray a nonstick wok or frying pan with oil and heat. Cook fish in 2 batches over medium-high heat for 3 minutes or until browned and tender; set aside. Reheat wok, add garlic, ginger, lemongrass and onion; stirfry for 2 minutes or until soft. Add bok choy, broccoli and capsicum and stirfry until tender but still crisp. Combine sauces and vinegar, and stir into wok. Add fish to wok and reheat. Remove from heat and stir in bean sprouts. Serve immediately over noodles.

ANALYSIS		4		6
Energy (kJ Cal)	2295	548	1530	365
◼ Carb (g)		65		43
◼ Prot (g)		49		33
◼ Fat (g)		10		6
◾ Fibre, Iron, Vitamin C, Zinc				

Preparation time: 10 minutes
Cooking time: 10 minutes

stirfry fish with lemongrass & asian greens

butter chicken with vegetables

mary's peppered beef & vegetables

butter chicken with vegetables Serves 4-6 ❋

2 cups basmati rice
olive or canola oil spray
500 g chicken breast fillets, cut into cubes
1 onion, sliced
1 sachet MAGGI TASTE OF ASIA Butter Chicken
1 tablespoon tomato paste
375 ml CARNATION Light and Creamy Evaporated Milk
1 teaspoon coconut essence
1 cup MAGGI All Natural Chicken Liquid Stock
2 teaspoons brown sugar
300 g orange sweet potato, diced
200 g snow peas, halved
1 bunch asparagus, sliced
50 g toasted flaked almonds
2 tablespoons fresh coriander leaves

Cook rice in a large saucepan of boiling water for about 12 minutes or until tender. Drain well. Spray a nonstick wok or frying pan with oil and heat. Cook chicken in 2 batches over high heat until browned. Remove from wok. Add onion, spice sachet and 3 tablespoons water and cook over medium heat for 3 minutes or until onion is soft. Stir in tomato paste, milk, coconut essence, stock, sugar and sweet potato and cook, covered, for 10 minutes or until sweet potato is tender. Add chicken, snow peas and asparagus and cook, uncovered, for 5 minutes or until green vegetables are tender but still crisp. Serve on rice, sprinkled with toasted almonds and fresh coriander leaves.

ANALYSIS	4	6
Energy (kJ Cal)	3318 793	2212 528
▪ Carb (g)	113	75
▪ Prot (g)	49	33
▪ Fat (g)	16	11
▪ Calcium, Iron, Vitamin C, Zinc		

HINT: *This recipe freezes well. Vary the vegetables with bamboo shoots, zucchini, pumpkin and peas.*

Preparation time: 20 minutes
Cooking time: 35 minutes

mary's peppered beef & vegetables Serves 4-6 ❋

2 cups jasmine rice
olive or canola oil spray
500 g rump steak, cut into thin strips
2 teaspoons freshly cracked black pepper
1 teaspoon crushed garlic
3 spring onions, sliced
500 g packet frozen mixed stirfry vegetables (e.g. broccoli, corn, sugar snap peas and carrot)
1 bunch baby bok choy, coarsely chopped
3 tablespoons MAGGI Oyster Sauce
1 teaspoon honey
40 g blanched almonds
½ cup fresh coriander leaves

Cook rice in a large saucepan of boiling water for about 12 minutes or until tender. Drain well. Spray a nonstick wok or frying pan with oil and heat. Stirfry meat and pepper in 2 batches over high heat for 2–3 minutes or until well browned and tender. Remove from wok. Reheat wok, add garlic and spring onion and stirfry for 1 minute or until spring onion is soft. Add remaining vegetables and stirfry for about 5 minutes or until tender but still crisp. Add oyster sauce and honey to wok and stir through. Return beef to the wok and stir until heated through. Stir in nuts and coriander leaves. Serve immediately over rice.

ANALYSIS	4	6
Energy (kJ Cal)	2899 693	1933 462
▪ Carb (g)	101	68
▪ Prot (g)	41	27
▪ Fat (g)	13	9
▪ Iron, Zinc		

HINT: *Do not thaw frozen vegetables before adding to the wok or they will make the stirfry watery.*

Preparation time: 10 minutes
Cooking time: 25 minutes

MARY GRIGSON ~ mountain biking
mary's peppered beef & vegetables
Greatest sporting achievement:
Four-times Australian Mountain Bike Champion 1998-2001, 6th in mountain bike event at 2000 Olympics in Sydney.
Favourite cooking style:
Baking bread.
My contribution to Survival 2:
The realities of living 'on the road' are that you need to be able to cook in one pan with limited ingredients and flavouring condiments. This stirfry recipe is perfectly simple and perfectly delicious.

sweet & sour pork

sweet & sour pork   Serves 4-6 ✳

2 cups jasmine rice
olive or canola oil spray
500 g lean pork fillet, cut into thin strips
1 onion, sliced
1 small red capsicum, chopped
1 small green capsicum, chopped
1 carrot, sliced
440 g can pineapple pieces, drained and juices reserved
¼ cup tomato sauce
1 tablespoon MAGGI Chilli & Garlic Sauce
2 tablespoons white vinegar
1 tablespoon cornflour
coriander leaves, to garnish

Cook rice in a large saucepan of boiling water for about 12 minutes or until tender. Drain well. Spray a nonstick wok or frying pan with oil and heat. Add pork and cook in batches for 2–3 minutes over high heat, until browned and cooked through but tender; set aside. Reheat wok, add onion with 1 tablespoon water, and stirfry until golden. Add capsicum and carrot and stirfry until tender. Place pineapple juice, tomato sauce, chilli and garlic sauce, vinegar and cornflour in a jug and whisk until smooth. Return pork to wok, add the sauce and pineapple, stirring until sauce boils and thickens. Garnish with coriander leaves. Serve with rice.

ANALYSIS	4		6	
Energy (kJ Cal)	2643	631	1762	421
▪ Carb (g)		111		73
▪ Prot (g)		36		24
▪ Fat (g)		4		3
▪ Iron, Vitamin C, Zinc				

HINT: *Replace the pork with chicken breast fillets or cubed firm tofu.*

Preparation time: 15 minutes
Cooking time: 25 minutes

lachie's rogan josh with spinach & potatoes

Serves 4-6 ✳

2 cups basmati rice
olive or canola oil spray
500 g trim lamb fillet, cut into cubes
1 sachet MAGGI TASTE OF ASIA Beef Madras
1 onion, sliced
400 g can chopped tomatoes
300 g potatoes, peeled and cut into small cubes
200 g green beans, sliced
250 g English spinach, coarsely chopped
1 cup PETERS FARM No Fat Natural Yogurt
2 tablespoons toasted slivered almonds
8 poppadoms

LACHIE MILNE ~ slalom canoeing
lachie's rogan josh with spinach & potatoes
Greatest sporting moment:
Qualifying for World Cup Final (World Cup 1, 2000) in Penrith and finishing 12th.
Favourite food: My brother's Thai Green Curry.
My contribution to Survival 2:
This recipe is great as it provides the taste of a proper curry, really quickly. I'm always arriving home late from training and university—so a quick dinner is a good dinner.

Cook rice in a large saucepan of boiling water for about 12 minutes or until tender. Drain well. Spray a nonstick wok or frying pan with oil and heat. Cook lamb in 2 batches over medium–high heat until browned. Remove from wok. Add spice mix, onion and 3 tablespoons water and stirfry for 3 minutes or until onion is soft. Add tomato and potato and cook, covered, for 10 minutes or until potato is soft. Add lamb, beans and spinach and cook, covered, for 5 minutes or until vegetables are tender but still crisp. Stir through yogurt. Serve on rice with a dollop of yogurt and sprinkled with almonds. Cook poppadoms in the microwave following packet instructions, and serve on the side.

ANALYSIS	4		6	
Energy (kJ Cal)	2970	710	1980	473
▪ Carb (g)		107		72
▪ Prot (g)		46		31
▪ Fat (g)		10		6
▪ Iron, Vitamin C, Zinc				
▪ Calcium				

HINT: *This recipe freezes well without the spinach and yogurt. Add these after reheating.*

Preparation time: 10 minutes
Cooking time: 20 minutes

lachie's rogan josh with spinach & potatoes

vegetable tagine with couscous

chicken, cashew & hokkien noodle stirfry

vegetable tagine with couscous Serves 4-6 ❄

olive or canola oil spray
1 onion, chopped
1 teaspoon ground ginger
2 teaspoons ground paprika
pinch saffron threads
200 g sweet potato, chopped
200 g potato, chopped
2 cups frozen mixed vegetables (e.g. zucchini, beans, carrots)
400 g can crushed tomatoes
1 cup MAGGI All Natural Vegetable Liquid Stock
100 g dried prunes
1½ cups couscous
3 cups boiling MAGGI All Natural Vegetable Liquid Stock, extra
50 g toasted slivered almonds

Spray a large saucepan with oil and heat. Add onion and spices and cook over low heat until onion is soft and spices are fragrant. Add all the vegetables, stock and prunes, and simmer, uncovered, for 15 minutes or until potato is tender. Meanwhile, place couscous in a large bowl, pour boiling stock over it and allow to stand covered for 10 minutes or until all liquid is absorbed; toss lightly using a fork. Serve mounds of couscous topped with tagine and sprinkled with almonds. Garnish with flat-leaf parsley, if desired.

ANALYSIS	4		6	
Energy (kJ Cal)	2373	567	1582	378
Carb (g)		97		65
Prot (g)		21		14
Fat (g)		10		7
Fibre, Vitamin C				

HINT: *To increase protein levels, add chopped tofu or tempeh. This recipe freezes well. The prunes can be replaced with dried apricots.*

Preparation time: 15 minutes
Cooking time: 25 minutes

chicken, cashew & hokkien noodle stirfry

Serves 4-6 ❄

900 g hokkien noodles
olive or canola oil spray
400 g chicken breast fillet, thinly sliced
3 spring onions, sliced
1 carrot, sliced
1 small red capsicum, sliced
200 g snow peas, halved
400 g baby corn, cut lengthways
½ cup MAGGI Authentic Thai Sweet Chilli Sauce
2 tablespoons MAGGI Fish Sauce
2 tablespoons lemon juice
50 g toasted cashews

Place noodles in a large heatproof bowl and cover with boiling water. Leave to stand for 2 minutes, gently using a wooden spoon to separate strands. Drain well and set aside. Spray a wok with oil and heat. Add chicken and stirfry in batches until browned and tender; set aside. Add spring onion to the wok with 1 tablespoon water; stirfry until tender. Add vegetables and stirfry until soft, then add noodles. Add combined chilli sauce, fish sauce and lemon juice to wok and toss to coat noodles and vegetables. Cook for 3 minutes or until heated through. Return chicken to wok and cook for 2–3 minutes or until heated through. Serve sprinkled with cashews. Garnish with coriander leaves, if desired.

BRYONY DUUS ~ soccer
chicken, cashew & hokkien noodle stirfry
Greatest sporting moment: Coming back from two knee operations to play with the Matildas in the 2000 Olympics.
Favourite cooking style: I love to cook stirfries and experiment with different ingredients.
My contribution to Survival 2: This recipe is a no-fail stirfry. Just don't eat all the cashews before they are supposed to go in the recipe.

ANALYSIS	4		6	
Energy (kJ Cal)	2710	647	1806	431
Carb (g)		86		57
Prot (g)		40		27
Fat (g)		15		10
Fibre, Iron, Vitamin C, Zinc				

HINT: *This recipe is delicious as a cold salad.*

Preparation time: 20 minutes
Cooking time: 15 minutes

joe's tofu, vegetable & noodle green curry

joe's tofu, vegetable & noodle green curry

Serves 4-6 ✳

500 g dried rice vermicelli
olive or canola oil spray
1–2 tablespoons green curry paste (or red or yellow curry paste, if preferred)
2 slender eggplants, cut into thick slices
1 zucchini, sliced
350 g firm tofu, cubed
375 ml CARNATION Light and Creamy Evaporated Milk
1 teaspoon coconut essence
1 cup MAGGI All Natural Vegetable Liquid Stock
300 g broccoli, cut into florets
1 cup fresh or frozen peas
200 g can bamboo shoots, drained
1 cup sliced mushrooms
1 tablespoon lime juice
1 tablespoon brown sugar
2 tablespoons fresh coriander leaves, plus extra, to garnish

Cook vermicelli according to packet instructions; drain well. Spray a nonstick wok or frying pan with oil and heat. Stirfry curry paste over medium heat for 1–2 minutes until fragrant. Add eggplant and zucchini and stirfry for 2 minutes. Add tofu, milk, coconut essence and stock; bring to the boil. Reduce heat and simmer, uncovered, for 10 minutes. Add remaining ingredients except coriander for garnish. Cook for 5 minutes until vegetables are tender but still crisp. Serve curry over vermicelli in bowls, garnished with extra coriander.

ANALYSIS	4	6
Energy (kJ Cal)	2171 519	1448 346
▪ Carb (g)	75	50
▪ Prot (g)	32	21
▪ Fat (g)	10	7
▪ Calcium, Fibre, Iron, Vitamin C, Zinc		

Preparation time: 15 minutes
Cooking time: 25 minutes

JOE GAMBLES ~ triathlon
joe's tofu, vegetable & noodle green curry
Greatest sporting moment:
2nd Junior Male at 2000 World Triathlon Championships, Perth.
Favourite recipe/cooking style:
I love oven-baked vegetables like potatoes and pumpkin.
My contribution to Survival 2:
I follow a vegetarian lifestyle as I love animals too much to eat them. This dish is rich in carbohydrate and protein, but most importantly, has interesting flavours.

pork, pineapple & peanut curry Serves 4-6 ✳

2 cups jasmine rice
olive or canola oil spray
1 onion, cut into wedges
2 tablespoons red curry paste
375 ml can CARNATION Light and Creamy Evaporated Milk
1 teaspoon coconut essence
125 ml MAGGI All Natural Chicken Liquid Stock
1 teaspoon MAGGI Fish Sauce
4 kaffir lime leaves, thinly shredded
300 g Jap or butternut pumpkin, cut into small cubes
500 g pork fillets, cut into thin slices
200 g green beans, halved
200 g broccoli florets
450 g can pineapple pieces in natural juice, drained and juice reserved
1 tablespoon cornflour
50 g crushed peanuts or cashews

Cook rice in a large saucepan of boiling water for about 12 minutes or until tender. Drain well and set aside. Spray a nonstick wok or frying pan with oil and heat. Cook onion over medium heat for 3 minutes or until soft. Add curry paste and stirfry for 1 minute. Stir in milk, coconut essence, stock, fish sauce and kaffir lime. Bring to the boil. Add pumpkin and pork and simmer, uncovered, for 10 minutes. Add beans, broccoli and pineapple to curry; cook until tender. Blend cornflour with pineapple juice, add to curry and stir until sauce boils and thickens. Serve curry over rice topped with nuts. Garnish with shredded kaffir lime leaves, if desired.

ANALYSIS	4	6
Energy (kJ Cal)	3274 782	2183 521
▪ Carb (g)	115	77
▪ Prot (g)	52	34
▪ Fat (g)	12	8
▪ Calcium, Iron, Vitamin C, Zinc		

HINT: *This recipe freezes well; thicken with cornflour before reheating.*

Preparation time: 20 minutes
Cooking time: 25 minutes

pork, pineapple & peanut curry

michael's beef curry in a hurry

spicy vegetable filo roll

michael's beef curry in a hurry   Serves 4-6   ❄

2 cups basmati rice
olive or canola oil spray
500 g rump steak, sliced
1 onion, sliced
2 teaspoons curry powder (e.g. Madras-style blend)
375 ml CARNATION Light and Creamy Evaporated Milk
1 teaspoon coconut essence
1 cup MAGGI All Natural Beef Liquid Stock
300 g potatoes, cubed
200 g button mushrooms, quartered
150 g green beans, halved
1 red capsicum, sliced
1 tablespoon cornflour

Cook rice in a large saucepan of boiling water for 12 minutes or until tender. Drain well. Spray a nonstick wok or frying pan with oil and heat. Cook beef in 2 batches over high heat until browned. Remove from wok. Cook onion and curry powder over medium heat for 2 minutes or until onion is soft. Stir in milk, coconut essence and stock. Bring to simmer. Add potato and mushrooms and cook, uncovered, for 10 minutes, until potato is soft. Add beans and capsicum, and cook for 5 minutes, until tender but crisp. Blend cornflour with 2 tablespoons water. Add to curry, stirring until sauce boils and thickens slightly. Add beef and heat through. Serve with rice. Garnish with chervil, if desired.

HINT: *Most curries freeze well as the flavour develops on standing.*

Preparation time: 15 minutes
Cooking time: 30 minutes

ANALYSIS		4		6
Energy (kJ Cal)	2920	698	1947	456
▪ Carb (g)		108		72
▪ Prot (g)		48		32
▪ Fat (g)		8		5
▪ Iron, Vitamin C, Zinc				
▪ Calcium				

spicy vegetable filo roll   Serves 4-6   ❄

olive or canola oil spray
2 onions, thinly sliced
2 tablespoons brown mustard seeds
1 tablespoon curry powder
2 carrots, sliced
2 zucchini, sliced
600 g potatoes, peeled and cubed
1 kg pumpkin, peeled and cubed
2 cups fresh or frozen peas
2 cups (500 ml) MAGGI All Natural Vegetable Liquid Stock
16 sheets filo pastry
2 tablespoons sesame seeds

Spray a large nonstick frying pan with oil and heat. Cook onion, mustard seeds and curry powder over medium heat until onion is soft. Add vegetables and cook for 3 minutes, stirring well to combine. Add stock and cook, uncovered, for 20–25 minutes or until vegetables are soft and liquid has evaporated. Remove from pan; allow to cool completely. Preheat oven to 220°C (425°F). Place one pastry sheet on a flat surface, lightly spray with oil and place another sheet on top: continue layering until you have eight layers. Place half the filling along one edge, with a 2-cm border at each end. Fold in ends and roll up to enclose. Repeat using remaining pastry and filling. Place rolls on a nonstick baking tray, seal side down, lightly spray with oil and sprinkle with sesame seeds. Bake for 20 minutes or until crisp and golden. Serve cut into slices, with a green salad.

HINT: *A great recipe for using leftovers. Freeze rolls, uncooked, tightly wrapped in plastic; thaw and bake.*

Preparation time: 25 minutes
Cooking time: 50 minutes

ANALYSIS		4		6
Energy (kJ Cal)	2034	486	1356	324
▪ Carb (g)		80		53
▪ Prot (g)		24		16
▪ Fat (g)		8		5
▪ Fibre, Iron, Vitamin C, Zinc				

MICHAEL KLIM ~ swimming
michael's beef curry in a hurry
Most memorable sporting moment: The 4x100m relay at the 2000 Olympics in Sydney—especially the air guitar.
Greatest sporting achievement: Breaking the 100m butterfly record.
My contribution to Survival 2: One night, some of my team mates and I were on our way home, exhausted after training. We ran into Bipin (AIS cook) and he came home and cooked us a sensational, authentic curry. Now, with the new Survival, we can cook our own tasty but healthy curries in a flash.

spicy lamb wraps

ADAM CAPORN ~ basketball
pork with spicy plum sauce
Greatest sporting moment:
Playing for Australia in the
Albert Schweitzer Tournament.
Favourite food: Steak and
vegetables, I like my food simple.
My contribution to Survival 2:
I like my meat and this meal
enables me to combine it with
noodles, providing me with
replacement carbohydrate after
each day's training. It also
tastes pretty good!

spicy lamb wraps   Serves 4-6

500 g trim lamb loin
1 teaspoon minced garlic
1 teaspoon ground cinnamon
¼ teaspoon ground allspice
1 tablespoon honey
1 tablespoon lemon juice
olive or canola oil spray
4 rounds Lebanese bread
100 g low-fat hummus
2 cups shredded lettuce
200 g tabbouli (see Hints & Tips, page 91 for recipe)
130 g can corn kernels, drained
2 tomatoes, halved and sliced
1 red onion, thinly sliced
⅓ cup MAGGI Chilli Sauce

Place lamb, garlic, spices, honey and juice in a nonmetallic bowl, toss to coat lamb, then marinate 10 minutes. Spray a nonstick frying pan with oil and heat. Cook lamb in 2 batches over high heat until browned and tender. Remove from pan. Allow to stand for 5 minutes before slicing thinly. Place bread on a flat surface. Divide hummus between bread and spread evenly to cover the centre of the bread. Top with lettuce, tabbouli, corn and tomato. Arrange lamb along centre, top with onion and roll up firmly to enclose. Place wrap in a heated sandwich press and cook for 3–5 minutes or until bread is crisp. Or, grill lightly on both sides. Cut in half and drizzle with chilli sauce. Serve with salad.

ANALYSIS	4		6	
Energy (kJ Cal)	2514	601	1676	400
▦ Carb (g)		85		57
▦ Prot (g)		40		27
▦ Fat (g)		11		7
▦ Iron, Zinc				

Preparation time:
10 minutes + 10 minutes marinating
Cooking time: 10 minutes

pork with spicy plum sauce   Serves 4-6 ❋

900 g hokkien noodles
olive or canola oil spray
500 g lean pork fillet, cut into thin strips
1 tablespoon grated fresh ginger
1 onion, sliced
1 bunch asparagus, cut into short lengths
200 g broccoli, cut into florets
1 cup chopped red capsicum
200 g snow peas, halved
⅓ cup plum sauce
2 tablespoons MAGGI Extra Hot Chilli Sauce
⅓ cup reduced-salt soy sauce

Place noodles in a large heatproof bowl and cover with boiling water. Leave to stand for 2 minutes, gently using a wooden spoon to separate strands. Drain well. Spray a wok with oil and heat. Add pork and stirfry over high heat until browned and cooked through, then set aside. Add ginger and onion to wok with 1 tablespoon water and stirfry until golden. Add asparagus, broccoli, capsicum and snow peas and stirfry until bright green and tender. Put sauces in a jug and whisk to combine. Add to wok, stirring over high heat until sauce thickens slightly. Return pork to wok and cook for 2 minutes or until heated through. Serve noodles topped with pork. Garnish with chervil and chopped chives, if desired.

HINT: *Vary with thinly sliced chicken breasts instead of pork.*

Preparation time: 15 minutes
Cooking time: 15 minutes

ANALYSIS	4		6	
Energy (kJ Cal)	2211	528	1474	352
▦ Carb (g)		76		51
▦ Prot (g)		43		29
▦ Fat (g)		5		3
▦ Iron, Vitamin C, Zinc				

pork with spicy plum sauce

bakes&
grills

1

bakes & grills

The Aussie barbecue and baked dinner are icons of our national culture, but often these are high-fat low-carbohydrate affairs. Our recipes take a different approach—ensuring a balanced meal without compromising on flavour.

At the AIS, barbecues are designed to be greatly enjoyable, and balanced—with smaller serves of lean meat, accompanied by high-carbohydrate foods such as bread, rolls, rice, pasta and potato salads (made with low-fat dressings), tossed salad and a fruit platter.

Our recipes are also suitable for indoor hot plates or the griller, which is part of the oven. A grill plate that is slotted or sloping allows fat to drain away, while a light spray of canola or olive oil on the plate ensures that grilling is a low-fat cooking method.

Baked dishes are often high in fat due to a thick covering of cheese, resulting in a layer of oil on top of the dish after cooking. However, you can still 'gratinate' or brown the top of a dish with reduced-fat or light cheese in smaller quantities. Compare these:

- 1 cup (120 g) regular grated cheese = 40 g fat
- $^{1}/_{2}$ cup (60 g) light (25% fat) grated cheese = 15 g fat
- 2 tablespoons Parmesan cheese = 4 g fat

Therefore, to reduce fat content without compromising on taste, use a strongly flavoured cheese like Parmesan—2 tablespoons Parmesan (4 g fat) can replace $^{1}/_{2}$ cup grated cheese (20 g fat).

Low-fat baking is easy. Make sure you trim all visible fat from the meat (see Hints & Tips), then place the meat on a wire rack in a baking tray. This allows fat to drip from the meat into the tray and not be re-absorbed during cooking. You can subtly flavour the meat by placing herbs in the tray—rosemary or mint with lamb, garlic cloves with beef, or thyme with chicken, for example.

If you want to bake quickly, use a microwave oven to partially cook the dish, then finish it conventionally. Combining cooking in microwave and conventional ovens speeds up the process without losing the golden finish and taste of baked food (see Hints & Tips). After microwaving, place the dish in a preheated conventional oven, as directed by the recipe, for 10–15 minutes, or until the dish is cooked and golden brown on top.

hints & tips

▶ Trim visible fat from meat before baking or grilling—even if you plan to avoid the fat once cooked, some of it will remain. Lean meat, however, is more likely to dry out, so marinate the meat to keep it moist. When baking meat, place liquid such as water or fruit juice in the baking tray under the rack, or cover it with aluminium foil and remove foil only for the last 10-15 minutes of baking.

▶ Foil can also be used to protect the more delicate parts of meat while baking. For example, place small pieces of foil on the chicken breast, tips of wings and drumsticks.

▶ If using a fan-forced or convection oven for baking, reduce the temperature stated in the recipe by 10-20°C for most foods. You may also need to do this with gas ovens.

▶ Microwave ovens vary in power output but in general, 1 minute in the microwave equals 4 minutes in a conventional oven. You need to experiment with your microwave as it is very easy to overcook food. Also, food continues to cook for 5-10 minutes after the actual microwaving so you must allow for this. It is better to undercook food in the microwave.

▶ When using wooden skewers, soak the skewers in warm water for about 30 minutes before preparation of food and cooking. If cooking over open flames, you may also need to protect the ends of the skewers with foil.

▶ Always clean a grill plate or barbecue hot plate before using to ensure hygienic cooking, but also to avoid fat from prior cooking being absorbed into your food. Better still, clean the plate after you've used it. To clean easily and without harsh chemicals, just cut a lemon in half and rub it over the hot plate. Be careful not to get burnt as the juice creates steam.

▶ If you're at a barbecue or dinner with no choice about the menu, always balance the meal with a good serve of bread, plenty of vegetables or salad, and half the usual serve of meat, fish or chicken. Take fresh bread along to ensure you will be able to meet your nutritional needs (choose specialty types).

▶ Bread is a great source of carbohydrate, much like pasta and rice—in fact, 1 cup cooked rice or pasta is similar in carbohydrate and kilojoule value to 4 slices of bread. Choose specialty bread that is eaten in larger portions such as cobs, pull-aparts, focaccia, plaits and pide rather than sandwich-style thin-sliced bread.

beef & vegetable satay sticks   Serves 4

500 g rump steak, cut into 2-cm cubes
6 spring onions, cut into 3-cm lengths
1 large red capsicum, cut into cubes
200 g button mushrooms, halved
2 large zucchini, cut into thick slices
2 tablespoons oil-free French dressing
1 teaspoon honey

Soak bamboo skewers in water for 10 minutes to prevent them from burning under the grill. Thread the steak, spring onion, capsicum, mushrooms and zucchini onto the skewers. Place skewers on a foil-lined grill tray and baste with combined dressing and honey. Cook under a preheated grill on high, or on a barbecue hot plate, basting and turning a couple of times during cooking until the beef is tender. Serve skewers with a salad or wrapped in a piece of Lebanese bread with rocket. Drizzle with your favourite sauce. Serve with salad on the side, if desired.

ANALYSIS	4
Energy (kJ Cal)	2675 639
Carb (g)	90
Prot (g)	45
Fat (g)	11
Fibre, Iron, Vitamin C, Zinc	

HINT: *Any lean meat can be used to make the satay. Vegetarians can use firm tofu diced into cubes.*

Preparation time: 15 minutes
Cooking time: 10 minutes

beef & vegetable satay sticks

ALEXANDRA CROAK ~ gymnastics
beef & vegetable sate sticks
Greatest sporting moment:
2000 Olympic Games—Apparatus Beam—absolutely perfect.
Favourite recipe/cooking style:
AIS Dining Hall Beef Burrito.
My contribution to Survival 2:
I am hooked on anything that comes on a skewer. These sate sticks are fun to make and are great for a barbecue lunch. I always wrap mine in Lebanese bread and add extra salad— so yum!

fish in foil   Serves 4

4 x 150 g salmon fillets, skin removed
4 thin slices ginger
1 stalk lemongrass, finely sliced
3 spring onions, sliced
1 red capsicum, thinly sliced
1 carrot, cut into thin strips
1 teaspoon sesame oil
3 tablespoons lime juice
2 tablespoons MAGGI Authentic Thai Sweet Chilli Sauce
1 tablespoon MAGGI Fish Sauce
500 g baby bok choy, halved
fresh coriander leaves, to serve

Cut four x 30-cm squares of aluminium foil. Place fish on the centre of the foil, top with ginger and lemongrass and finely sliced vegetables. Place sesame oil, lime juice, chilli sauce and fish sauce in a jug and whisk to combine. Fold up the edges of the foil so none of the liquid can flow away and then carefully pour the sauce over the fish. Loosely seal the fish in foil, then place in a large bamboo steamer over a wok of simmering water (making sure the base of the steamer does not come into contact with the water). Cover the steamer and cook fish in foil for 10–15 minutes or until nearly cooked through. Place the bok choy in a separate steamer on top of the fish and cook, covered, for 5 minutes or until tender. Serve the fish parcels on top of the steamed bok choy, garnished with coriander. Serve with steamed jasmine rice.

HINT: *If you don't have a wok and steamer, these parcels can be cooked in the microwave but use baking paper in place of the foil. They can also be cooked on a baking tray in a preheated 180°C (350°F) oven for 10–15 minutes or until tender.*

ANALYSIS	4
Energy (kJ Cal)	3098 740
Carb (g)	112
Prot (g)	41
Fat (g)	13
Iron, Vitamin C, Zinc	

Preparation time: 20 minutes
Cooking time: 20 minutes

fish in foil

chicken burger

taylor-made lentil patties

chicken burger Makes 12 ❊

Chicken patties:
1 kg chicken mince
½ cup grated carrot
½ cup finely chopped onion
½ cup diced celery

hamburger buns, split
English spinach leaves
tomato slices
snow pea sprouts
strips of chargrilled capsicum
MAGGI Authentic Thai Sweet Chilli Sauce

To make chicken patties, place chicken, carrot, onion and celery in a bowl and mix to combine. Divide mixture into 12 portions and shape each portion into a flat patty. Cook patties on a foil-lined grill tray under a preheated grill on medium–high, or on a barbecue hot plate, for 5 minutes on each side, or until golden brown on both sides and cooked through. Meanwhile, toast the bread rolls. Assemble rolls with English spinach, tomato, cooked chicken patty, snow pea sprouts and capsicum. Serve with sweet chilli sauce on the side.

ANALYSIS	12
Energy (kJ Cal)	1580 377
■ Carb (g)	45
■ Prot (g)	24
■ Fat (g)	11
■ Fibre, Iron, Vitamin C, Zinc	

Preparation time: 15 minutes
Cooking time: 10 minutes

taylor-made lentil patties Serves 4-6 ❊

1 large potato, cubed
2 cups cooked brown or green lentils
1 cup fresh breadcrumbs
1 egg, lightly beaten
¼ cup sesame seeds
¼ cup sunflower seeds
½ cup finely chopped almonds
1 onion, finely chopped
1 teaspoon minced garlic
2 tablespoons chopped fresh flat-leaf parsley
pepper, to taste
olive or canola oil spray

RYAN TAYLOR ~ athletics
taylor-made lentil patties
Greatest sporting moment:
Scoring a hole-in-one on the
golf course—magical!
Favourite food: Pizza ...
and lots of it!
My contribution to Survival 2:
I have recently become a
vegetarian, much to the
disappointment of my father
who is a butcher. I host regular
barbecues at home and now
include lentil burgers. I've
found my running mates are
getting into them, too!

Cook potato in a large saucepan of boiling water until soft, drain and mash until smooth. Add lentils, breadcrumbs, egg, sesame and sunflower seeds, almonds, onion, garlic, parsley and pepper. Mix well. Divide mixture into portions and form into patties. Spray a nonstick frying pan with oil and heat. Fry the patties over moderate heat for about 5 minutes on each side, or until crisp and golden on the outside and heated through. Serve with a crusty wholemeal bread roll and salad.

ANALYSIS	4	6
Energy (kJ Cal)	2225 710	1773 759
■ Carb (g)	54	49
■ Prot (g)	24	19
■ Fat (g)	24	17
■ Fibre, Iron, Zinc		

HINT: *These patties freeze well uncooked; thaw before cooking. Vary with a mix of red and green lentils. Canned lentils may be used to save time.*

Preparation time: 20 minutes
Cooking time: 15 minutes

sandwiches

club sandwich

vegetarian roll-up

layered ricotta & vegetable cob

steak sandwich

sandwiches

The tradition of breadmaking goes back thousands of years and today we have an infinite range. From rolls and pockets to pides and plaits, made of wheat, rye or rice flour, with all sorts of delicious and beneficial additions, the choice of bread is endless.

All forms of bread are great fuel sources—low in fat and high in carbohydrate. The range is enormous, and even the modern sandwich loaf has many variations. Bread can be flavoured, too, or contain fruit, nuts or seeds. It can also be made without yeast and allowed to ferment naturally, as in sourdough. Whatever your favourite bread, the possibilities for fillings are only limited by your imagination. Here are a few suggestions to get you started.

Gourmet sandwich fillings / With gourmet fillings, use your imagination to invent new creations. Don't forget to use leftovers.

- Vegie wrap—fill flatbread with low-fat hummus and fresh raw or blanched vegetables (also include fresh or dried fruit).
- BBQ bagel—barbecued meat or chicken fillet and capsicum with Cajun spices, served hot on rocket leaves and sliced cucumber, topped with natural yogurt, in a bagel.
- Fruit & herb—cottage cheese mixed with herbs (e.g. chopped mint and oregano) spread on fruit bread, with slices of fruit on top. Sprinkle with chopped nuts, if desired.
- Fillet of fish—flour and season a fish fillet, grill, and place on a soft damper or bap-style roll with butter lettuce and low-fat tartare sauce (see Hints & Tips).

Fast, nutritious sandwich fillings / For quick and tasty fillings, try chicken with corn relish; cold roast beef, horseradish and rocket; smoked salmon with watercress; cottage cheese with chopped walnuts and raisins, or mixed with grated carrot, corn kernels and sliced cucumber; curried egg with cucumber and snow pea sprouts; grilled eggplant, sliced tomatoes and olives, sprinkled with grated Parmesan; double-smoked ham, asparagus and semidried tomatoes; turkey breast slices, cranberry sauce and a slice of camembert; peanut butter and salad.

hints & tips

➤ Stock up on bread when it's on special—it freezes really well. If you want a few slices for sandwiches or toast, freeze bread in smaller quantities. Make sure you wrap it, or put it into airtight bags. Pre-slice rolls so that they are easy to fill even when still frozen.

➤ You can also make up sandwiches and rolls with fillings such as deli meats and cheese, then freeze them complete. It's a great way to store them, they thaw out quickly, and will be as fresh as when you made them.

➤ For spreading on bread to add flavour or help keep it moist, there are many options other than butter or margarine—try low-fat versions of mayonnaise, ricotta, cottage or cream cheese, or dips; or avocado, peanut butter, relishes, chutneys and sauces.

➤ Toast sandwiches to use bread that is no longer fresh. Just make your sandwich as usual, heat a nonstick frying pan, spray it with oil and cook the sandwich until golden brown. The trick is to flip it without losing the filling! Or, use a sandwich maker sprayed with oil (don't butter the outside of the bread).

➤ Great flavour boosters for fillings include horseradish, relishes, chutneys, salsa, pickles, mustard and fresh herbs. To make low-fat tartare-style sauce, mix natural yogurt with lemon juice, capers and chopped parsley.

➤ Breadmakers allow you to bake fresh bread at home, as well as providing many possibilities to create your own flavours. To rejuvenate homemade bread, place it back into the breadmaker on the warm-hold cycle—the bread will emerge again as if it had just been baked. Or, warm it in a preheated 180°C (350°F) oven for a few minutes.

RECIPE FOR TABBOULI

2 cups boiling water
1 cup burghul
2 spring onions, chopped
2 medium tomatoes, diced
1/2 cup chopped mint
2 cups chopped parsley
1/4 cup lemon juice (juice of 1 lemon)
ground black pepper, to taste

Soak burghul in boiling water for 15 minutes. Squeeze out excess water. Combine burghul with all other ingredients. Mix well.

ANALYSIS	4		6	
Energy (kJ **Cal**)	860	205	573	137
Carb (g)		41		28
Prot (g)		6		4
Fat (g)		<1		1
Fibre, Iron, Vitamin C				

club sandwich Serves 4

8 thick slices wholemeal bread, toasted
4 thick slices rye bread, toasted
3 tablespoons low-fat mayonnaise
8 baby cos lettuce leaves
150 g barbecued chicken (white meat only), or shaved
  strips of cooked low-fat turkey breast
4 slices reduced-fat cheese
1 large tomato, sliced
50 g shaved reduced-fat ham
1 Lebanese cucumber, cut into very thin strips lengthways

Trim crust off bread. Lightly spread with mayonnaise. To assemble, place lettuce leaves on wholemeal bread slices, top with chicken, followed by a slice of rye bread, cheese, tomato, ham and cucumber. Finish with wholemeal bread.

ANALYSIS	4
Energy (kJ Cal)	2077 496
▦ Carb (g)	56
▦ Prot (g)	33
▦ Fat (g)	15
▦ Calcium, Fibre, Iron, Zinc	

Preparation time:
10 minutes
Total cooking: nil

layered ricotta & vegetable cob

Serves 4

1 wholemeal cob loaf
olive or canola oil spray
2 red capsicums, halved and seeded
2 zucchini, cut into thin slices lengthways
150 g low-fat ricotta cheese
130 g can creamed corn
130 g can corn kernels, drained
2 tablespoons snipped fresh chives
2 hard-boiled eggs, chopped
50 g baby spinach leaves

Preheat oven to 200°C (400°F). Slice top off cob and scoop out bread, leaving a 1-cm border on the inside. Place scooped bread in a food processor and process to form breadcrumbs. Spray a chargrill pan or barbecue plate with oil and heat. Grill capsicum until the skin blisters and blackens, transfer to a plastic bag and allow to cool, then peel away the skin. Grill zucchini on both sides until tender. Combine ricotta, creamed corn, corn kernels, chives, breadcrumbs and egg. Spread a quarter of the mixture over the cob base. Top with a quarter of the spinach, a quarter of the capsicum and a quarter of the zucchini. Repeat layers until you have used all the ingredients, then lightly press down and replace the top of the cob loaf. Bake for 20 minutes or until the outside is crisp and filling is heated through. Allow to cool, then slice into wedges and serve with salad.

HINT: *Drain the ricotta well before using—this will help prevent the cob from becoming soggy.*

ANALYSIS	4
Energy (kJ Cal)	2339 559
▦ Carb (g)	82
▦ Prot (g)	27
▦ Fat (g)	13
▦ Calcium, Fibre, Iron, Vitamin C, Zinc	

Preparation time:
15 minutes
Total cooking:
30 minutes

vegetarian roll-up Serves 4

4 wholemeal Lebanese bread rounds
400 g can chickpeas, rinsed and drained
1 teaspoon ground cumin
1/2 teaspoon ground paprika
1 tablespoon lemon juice
2 tablespoons PETERS FARM No Fat Natural Yogurt
1 cup shredded lettuce
200 g tabbouli (see Hints & Tips, page 91 for recipe)
1 yellow capsicum, thinly sliced
2 tomatoes, cut into wedges
1 red onion, thinly sliced
2 tablespoons MAGGI Chilli & Garlic Sauce

Lay out bread on a flat surface. Place chickpeas in a bowl and coarsely mash. Add cumin, paprika, lemon juice and yogurt and mix to combine. Divide chickpea mixture among bread rounds and spread to cover the centre. Top with lettuce, tabbouli, yellow capsicum, tomato and red onion and drizzle with chilli sauce. Roll up to enclose. Cut the roll in half to serve, with salad.

ANALYSIS	4
Energy (kJ Cal)	1865 445
▦ Carb (g)	80
▦ Prot (g)	19
▦ Fat (g)	5
▦ Fibre, Iron, Vitamin C, Zinc	

Preparation time:
10 minutes
Total cooking: nil

steak sandwich Serves 4

olive or canola oil spray
200 g button mushrooms, sliced
3 tablespoons balsamic vinegar
2 onions, thinly sliced
1 teaspoon brown sugar
4 fillet steaks, flattened slightly
8 slices ciabatta or slices of sourdough
50 g mixed salad leaves
2 tomatoes, thinly sliced
300 g can beetroot slices, drained
50 g snow pea sprouts

Spray a nonstick frying pan with oil and heat. Add mushrooms and 1 tablespoon balsamic vinegar and cook over high heat until browned and tender. Remove from pan. Add onion, remaining balsamic vinegar and sugar and cook over low-medium heat for 10 minutes or until caramelised. Remove from pan. Clean pan, respray with oil and heat. Cook steaks over high heat for 3 minutes on each side, or to your liking. Toast bread until golden brown on both sides. To assemble, on a slice of bread, place salad leaves, tomato, onion, steak, beetroot, snow pea sprouts and mushrooms. Top with another slice of bread.

HINT: *Try these sandwiches with thin veal escalopes or flattened chicken breasts instead of steak.*

ANALYSIS	4
Energy (kJ Cal)	2246 536
▦ Carb (g)	69
▦ Prot (g)	41
▦ Fat (g)	10
▦ Fibre, Iron, Zinc	

Preparation time:
10 minutes
Total cooking:
20 minutes

pizza

sweet potato, chicken & banana pizza

spinach, potato & pesto pizzas

aussie pizzas

baby octopus pizza

pizza

Athletes love pizza so much that the AIS Dining Hall is set up so they can prepare their own. Unfortunately, most commercial pizzas are high in fat. But, with a little imagination and quality ingredients, your pizzas can be high in carbohydrate, vitamins and minerals, and light in fat. With toppings, almost anything goes.

Pizza bases are widely available, fresh, frozen or refrigerated. Some are plain. Others have sauce. They also vary in size and weight, for example, a 30-cm base can weigh between 250 g and 500 g, depending on ingredients. To maximise carbohydrate intake, choose thick, heavy bases with a low-fat content. In our recipes, we use 350 g pizza bases with a fat content of 2.5 g per 100 g.

But don't be limited by standard pizza bases—almost any type of firm bread works well. Try Turkish or pitta bread, focaccias, English muffins or crumpets. And, if you're feeling really adventurous, make your own base (see Hints & Tips for recipes).

Pizzas need sauce for flavour. Traditionally, it's tomato-based but really the possibilities are endless. Try sauces such as satay, barbecue, plum, taco, chilli or Asian stirfry sauce. Pesto, relish and chutney work well, as do mashed vegetables, creamed corn or puréed fruit.

Almost anything in the fridge or cupboard can be added to a pizza. Try leftover cooked vegetables (especially pumpkin, potato and sweet potato) or grated fresh vegetables. Fruit works surprisingly well on both sweet and savoury pizzas. Canned tuna, salmon or sardines are other options. To boost carbohydrate levels in pizzas, add cooked pasta, kidney or baked beans, chickpeas, potato, corn, pineapple, mango or banana to the topping.

A topping of cheese should only be added for flavour and a golden finish—as a light sprinkle rather than a thick cover—and shouldn't be a main ingredient in the pizza. Always use reduced-fat cheeses (combining light tasty cheese and light mozzarella works well) but remember that even these are quite high in fat. Experiment with different cheeses—cottage, ricotta and reduced-fat fetta also make great pizza toppings. Sometimes, all you need is a very light sprinkle of Parmesan for flavour.

sweet potato, chicken & banana pizza   Serves 4 ❄

1 medium sweet potato, cubed
Turkish bread (or large pizza base or 4 small rounds
Lebanese bread)
½ cup tomato-based pasta sauce
2 spring onions, sliced
6 mushrooms, chopped
1 medium banana, chopped
90 g cooked chicken, chopped
ground black pepper
90 g grated reduced-fat cheese
(or low-fat fetta cheese, crumbled)
fresh basil leaves

Preheat oven to 220°C (425°F). Boil sweet potato until cooked but still firm. Or microwave, covered, on HIGH for 5–10 minutes. Spread Turkish bread with sauce and add all toppings except basil. Place on a nonstick baking tray. Bake for 10–20 minutes (depending on base), until cheese is golden. Sprinkle with basil and serve.

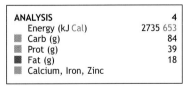

ANALYSIS		4
Energy (kJ Cal)	2079	497
■ Carb (g)		74
■ Prot (g)		26
■ Fat (g)		11
■ Calcium		

Preparation time:
15 minutes
Cooking time:
30 minutes

aussie pizzas   Serves 4 ❄

4 individual pizza bases (or 1 large base)
½ cup barbecue sauce
2–4 teaspoons crushed garlic (optional)
1 medium onion, chopped
180 g reduced-fat leg ham, chopped
80 g lean bacon, fat trimmed
1 medium red capsicum, chopped
1½ cups sliced mushrooms
2 eggs, lightly beaten
100 g grated reduced-fat mozzarella cheese

Preheat oven to 220°C (425°F). Place bases on a nonstick baking tray. Combine sauce and garlic and spread over bases, leaving a 1-cm border, then add toppings. Drizzle with egg, sprinkle with cheese and bake for 15–20 minutes, until egg sets.

ANALYSIS		4
Energy (kJ Cal)	2735	653
■ Carb (g)		84
■ Prot (g)		39
■ Fat (g)		18
■ Calcium, Iron, Zinc		

HINT: *Add canned pineapple for sweetness.*

Preparation time:
15 minutes
Cooking time:
15-20 minutes

spinach, potato & pesto pizzas

Serves 4

2 large potatoes, peeled
4 individual pizza bases
2 tablespoons pesto
100 g cherry tomatoes, halved
4 baby bocconcini cheese, sliced
50 g baby spinach leaves

Preheat oven to 210°C (415°F). Boil potatoes until just tender, drain and cut into thick slices. Place bases on a nonstick baking tray, spread with pesto and top with potato, tomato and cheese. Bake for 20 minutes or until bases are crisp and golden and cheese has melted. Top with spinach and serve immediately.

HINT: *Bocconcini are fresh mozzarella balls. Substitute 2 large-sized ones for 4 baby-sized.*

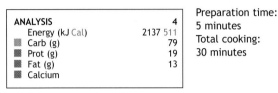

ANALYSIS		4
Energy (kJ Cal)	2137	511
■ Carb (g)		79
■ Prot (g)		19
■ Fat (g)		13
■ Calcium		

Preparation time:
5 minutes
Total cooking:
30 minutes

baby octopus pizza   Serves 4

¾ cup pumpkin, cubed
olive or canola oil spray
500 g clean fresh baby octopus (or prawns, if preferred)
1 tablespoon minced garlic
2 tablespoons chopped fresh chives
1 teaspoon minced chilli
1½ tablespoons balsamic vinegar
pinch of sugar
salt and pepper, to taste
2 tablespoons tomato paste
1 large precooked pizza base
2 tablespoons chopped fresh parsley

Preheat oven to 200°C (400°F). Microwave pumpkin on HIGH for 2 minutes, until tender. Spray a nonstick frying pan with oil and heat. Stirfry octopus for 1–2 minutes over high heat until tender. Combine pumpkin, octopus, garlic, chives, chilli, vinegar, sugar, salt and pepper in bowl. Spread tomato paste on base and add topping. Bake for 15–20 minutes until base is crisp and golden and topping heated through. Sprinkle with parsley and serve with salad.

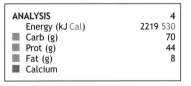

ANALYSIS		4
Energy (kJ Cal)	2219	530
■ Carb (g)		70
■ Prot (g)		44
■ Fat (g)		8
■ Calcium		

Preparation time:
15 minutes
Cooking time:
25 minutes

treats

treats

Something sweet at the end of a meal has been traditionally considered an indulgence. In fact, desserts and sweets can add valuable carbohydrate or important nutrients such as calcium. When smart choices are made, treats become a nutritional asset rather than just extra kilojoules.

Many recipes for treats and desserts call for large amounts of ingredients such as butter, oil and cream. With a few simple adjustments, however, most of these recipes can be transformed into high-carbohydrate, lower fat options. Even if you top your creation with a scoop of reduced-fat ice cream or a dash of low-fat custard, it should still fit within most kilojoule budgets.

Commercially available sweets do not fare so well. Pastries, doughnuts, ice cream, chocolate, pies and cakes are packed with carbohydrate, but also laden with fat. Don't be fooled by 'healthy' or 'all-natural' muffins, cakes and slices. These are usually high-fat snacks masquerading as healthy options. The best way to ensure treats are truly healthy and low in fat is to make your own.

It doesn't take hours in the kitchen or specialised cooking skills. Our recipes for desserts and treats all require minimal effort, use basic ingredients and are foolproof.

There are many low-fat packet mixes for desserts available— look for those that are 97 per cent fat-free—and these can be really convenient. Some, such as self-saucing pudding mixes, are already low in fat. Others can be easily modified to lower the fat content (use half the oil or margarine stated in the instructions and replace full-cream milk with skim milk). You can also make plain mixes interesting with your own additions (see Hints & Tips).

Some nutritious treats like oven-baked puddings, jellies and mousses take a little time to prepare, and it may even be best to make them a day in advance. When making jelly or mousse, allow time for setting. To speed up the process, pour the jelly or mousse into individual serving dishes such as glasses or cups.

hints & tips

➤ If you're planning a hot dessert, prepare it before the main meal and let it cook while you prepare and eat your meal. Use the oven timer so that you don't forget when the dessert is ready.

➤ Fruit crumble is a favourite in the AIS Dining Hall, and so easy to make, too. For the topping, mix $1^1/_2$ tablespoons melted margarine, 1 tablespoon brown sugar, 2 tablespoons golden syrup, $^3/_4$ cup plain flour and 1 cup cornflakes. Sprinkle over chopped fresh fruit or canned fruit such as pie apple. Bake in a preheated oven at 150°C (300°F) until golden brown. For a really easy crumble topping, use crushed cereal bars.

➤ Calcium is an essential nutrient for athletes. A low-fat custard, yogurt or dairy snack as dessert will boost your calcium and carbohydrate intake.

➤ If you don't have an electric beater or mixer to make the recipes, you can use a hand-held blender or beat (mix vigorously) the ingredients with a wooden spoon.

➤ Plain packet mixes (for example, cakes, muffins, pancakes and slices) can be made interesting with the addition of mashed banana, chopped apple and pear, dried fruit such as sultanas or dates, or a sprinkle of nutmeg and cinnamon.

➤ Rice pudding is a great way to use up leftover rice—just add a sprinkle of sugar and some low-fat milk and heat in the microwave.

➤ Premade custard is available in cartons or Tetra Paks® but if you prefer a thicker custard, make your own using custard powder. Mix 2 tablespoons custard powder, 1 tablespoon sugar and enough skim milk (about 2 tablespoons) to form a paste. Add 1 cup skim milk while stirring well. Microwave on MEDIUM for 5 minutes, stopping to stir after each minute.

➤ Adding icing to cakes and muffins often means adding a layer of fat. For a low-fat icing, mix 1 cup icing sugar with 1 teaspoon melted margarine. Add enough water, lemon juice or orange juice to form a spreadable consistency. For a low-fat cream-cheese icing, combine 2 tablespoons light cream cheese or 2 tablespoons light ricotta with 1 cup icing sugar. Add enough lemon or orange juice to form a spreadable consistency.

caramel raisin self-saucing pudding   Serves 4-6   ❋

1½ cups self-raising flour
½ cup brown sugar
½ cup raisins
1 egg
2 tablespoons margarine, melted
1 cup skim milk
2 teaspoons vanilla essence
PETERS Light and Creamy Vanilla Ice Cream (optional)

Sauce:
½ cup brown sugar
1½ tablespoons cornflour
2 tablespoons golden syrup
1¾ cups boiling water

Preheat oven to 180°C (350°F). Sift flour into a large bowl, stir in sugar and raisins and make a well in the centre. In another bowl, whisk together egg, margarine, milk and vanilla, then pour onto dry ingredients. Mix to combine. Place mixture into an 8-cup capacity ovenproof dish. To make the sauce, sprinkle the sugar over pudding mixture, then sift cornflour over it. Dissolve golden syrup in boiling water and gently pour over the back of a spoon onto pudding. Bake for 50 minutes or until a knife comes out clean when inserted into the pudding (but not through to the sauce). Serve with ice cream, if desired.

ANALYSIS		4	6
Energy (kJ Cal)		2243 536	1496 357
■ Carb (g)		107	71
■ Prot (g)		10	6
■ Fat (g)		9	6
▨ Calcium			

HINT: *This pudding is best eaten immediately. Serve with low-fat custard for extra calcium. Instead of skim milk, you can use 1 cup CARNATION Light and Creamy Evaporated Milk.*

Preparation time: 15 minutes
Cooking time: 50 minutes

caramel raisin self-saucing pudding

JIM FOWLIE ~ swimming coach
jim's blueberry hotcakes
Greatest sporting achievement:
Coaching Todd Pearson and Bill Kirby—two members of the swim team which won the Gold Medal in the 4x200m Relay at the 2000 Olympics in Sydney.
Favourite cooking style:
I'm the King of Barbecues.
Contribution to Survival 2:
I'm famous for my pancakes with the works—including bacon, eggs and Canadian maple syrup. This recipe is a little short on the 'works', but the upside is that it's healthy.

jim's blueberry hotcakes   Serves 4-6   ❋

200 g PETERS FARM No Fat Natural Yogurt
2 tablespoons honey
½ teaspoon ground cinnamon
2 cups self-raising flour
1 teaspoon baking powder
2 tablespoons caster sugar
1½ cups CARNATION Light and Creamy Evaporated Milk
2 eggs
2 teaspoons vanilla essence
300 g fresh or frozen blueberries
olive or canola oil spray

Place yogurt, honey and cinnamon in a small bowl, stir until combined. To make the hotcakes, sift flour and baking powder into a large bowl, stir in sugar and make a well in the centre. In another bowl, whisk together milk, eggs and vanilla and add to dry ingredients. Whisk until just combined—the mixture may be slightly lumpy, but don't overbeat or the hotcakes will be tough. Gently stir in blueberries. Spray a nonstick frying pan with oil and place over medium heat. Put ½ cup of batter into the pan, and cook for about 1½ minutes until bubbles appear on the surface. Turn over and cook a further 1 minute or until lightly golden underneath. Serve hotcakes with a dollop of yogurt mixture.

ANALYSIS		4	6
Energy (kJ Cal)		1908 456	1272 304
■ Carb (g)		87	58
■ Prot (g)		17	11
■ Fat (g)		4	3
▨ Calcium			

HINT: *Replace the blueberries with any other type of berry, or chopped banana, if you like. Or serve with plain yogurt and a drizzle of maple syrup.*

Preparation time: 10 minutes
Cooking time: 20 minutes

jim's blueberry hotcakes

golden syrup dumplings

alison's australian sticky date pudding

golden syrup dumplings Serves 4-6 ✳

1½ cups self-raising flour
2 teaspoons margarine
1 egg, lightly beaten
⅓ cup milk

600 ml carton low-fat prepared custard

Sauce:
2 cups water
1 cup caster sugar
⅓ cup golden syrup

Sift flour into a large bowl. Add margarine and rub in using fingertips, until mixture resembles fine breadcrumbs. Make a well in the centre. In a small jug, lightly beat egg and milk. Add to flour mixture, and mix using a butter knife until evenly moistened. Gather dough together gently. Pinch off portions and roll into walnut-sized balls (make 18 in total). Set aside. To make sauce, combine water, sugar and syrup in a wide saucepan and stir over medium heat without boiling until sugar dissolves. Increase heat to medium–high; bring to the boil. Add dumplings, cook for 8 minutes until increased in size and cooked through and syrup is reduced and thickened slightly. Serve dumplings drizzled with syrup and custard. Note: Take care when serving as the syrup will be extremely hot.

ANALYSIS		4		6
Energy (kJ Cal)	2617	625	1745	417
▪ Carb (g)		134		89
▪ Prot (g)		13		9
▪ Fat (g)		5		4
▪ Calcium				

Preparation time: 10 minutes
Cooking time: 10 minutes

alison's australian sticky date pudding

Serves 6-8 ✳

200 g dates, pitted and chopped
250 ml water
1 teaspoon bicarbonate of soda
1½ cups self-raising flour
½ cup brown sugar
1 egg
2 tablespoons canola oil
1 teaspoon vanilla essence
1 tablespoon custard powder
375 ml can CARNATION Light and Creamy Evaporated Milk
3 tablespoons brown sugar
3 tablespoons golden syrup

PETERS Light & Creamy Vanilla Ice Cream, to serve

Preheat oven to 180°C (350°F). Lightly grease a 20-cm round cake pan, and line base with baking paper. Place dates and water in small saucepan, bring to the boil, and remove from heat. Add bicarbonate of soda and stir well. Set aside. Sift flour into a large bowl, stir in sugar and make a well in the centre. In a small bowl, whisk egg, oil and vanilla, then add to flour mixture. Add date mixture and stir gently to combine. Pour into pan, and bake for 35 minutes or until a skewer or knife inserted into the cake comes out clean. Leave in pan for 5 minutes, then turn out. Meanwhile, to make the sauce, put custard powder in a small bowl and gradually add ⅓ cup milk, stirring until smooth. Place remaining milk in a small saucepan, and stir in sugar and golden syrup. Add custard mixture to saucepan, and stir over low heat until mixture boils and thickens. Serve pudding warm with sauce and a scoop of ice cream, if desired.

ANALYSIS		6		8
Energy (kJ Cal)	1708	408	1281	306
▪ Carb (g)		74		55
▪ Prot (g)		10		8
▪ Fat (g)		9		7
▪ Calcium				

HINT: *Store leftover pudding (without sauce) in an airtight container for up to 2 days. Leftover sauce should be kept in the fridge.*

Preparation time: 30 minutes
Cooking time: 35 minutes

ALISON WRIGHT ~ cycling
alison's australian sticky date pudding
Greatest sporting achievement:
Helping Anna Wilson to a World Cup win in 1999.
Favourite food:
Sticky date pudding.
Contribution to Survival 2:
When living in our European base in Italy, we often trade dinners with some of the locals. I need an authentic Australian dessert to show off against their tiramisu. A healthy sticky date pudding is a great way to fly the Aussie flag!

tropical trifle

tropical trifle   Serves 4-6

250 g packet sponge fingers (savoyardi biscuits)
2 x 450 g cans sliced mangoes, drained, juice reserved
170 g can passionfruit pulp
600 ml carton low-fat prepared custard
2 tablespoons desiccated coconut (optional)

Arrange sponge fingers over the base of a 6-cup capacity dish, breaking them as needed to fit in a single layer. Drizzle 3 tablespoons of reserved mango juice over sponge fingers. Spread over half the passionfruit pulp. Pour half the custard evenly over the top. Top with a layer of sliced mango. Repeat layers, finishing with sponge fingers (you may not need all the sponge fingers). Put coconut in a dry frying pan and stir over medium heat for about 1-2 minutes, until lightly golden. Transfer to a plate to cool, then sprinkle over trifle. Refrigerate for at least 1 hour before serving.

ANALYSIS	4	6
Energy (kJ Cal)	1927 460	1284 307
Carb (g)	87	58
Prot (g)	14	9
Fat (g)	7	4
Calcium, Fibre, Vitamin C		

HINT: *In place of the mango, use any canned fruit or fresh stone fruit in season. If using fresh fruit, add orange juice instead of reserved can juice. Keep in the fridge for up to 2 days.*

Preparation time:
15 minutes + 1 hour refrigeration
Cooking time: 2 minutes

carrot cake   Serves 12   ❋

1½ cups self-raising flour
1 cup wholemeal self-raising flour
1 teaspoon bicarbonate of soda
2 teaspoons mixed spice
1 cup brown sugar
2 eggs
2 tablespoons canola oil
½ cup skim milk
¾ cup prepared apple sauce
3 medium carrots (about 350 g), grated

Cream cheese frosting (optional):
½ cup light spreadable cream cheese
¼ cup icing sugar
1 teaspoon finely grated lemon rind

Preheat oven to 180°C (350°F). Lightly grease a 20-cm round cake pan, and line the base with baking paper. Sift flours, bicarbonate of soda and spice into a large bowl (tip in husks from flour, too), and stir in sugar. Make a well in the centre. In another bowl, whisk eggs, oil, milk and apple sauce using a fork, then add to flour mixture. Stir gently until just combined, then stir in carrot. Pour into prepared pan, and bake for about 70 minutes or until a skewer or knife inserted into the centre of the cake comes out clean. Leave in the pan for 5 minutes, before turning out on a wire rack to cool. If frosting, wait until cake is completely cool. To make frosting, put cream cheese in a bowl and sift icing sugar over it. Add lemon juice and stir until smooth.

HINT: *This cake keeps for up to 4 days in an airtight container. If frosted, keep in the fridge. Alternatively, cut unfrosted cake into portions, wrap tightly in layers of plastic wrap and freeze for up to 2 months. One piece will take about 2 hours to thaw at room temperature. Instead of using skim milk, you may use ½ cup CARNATION Light and Creamy Evaporated Milk.*

ANALYSIS	12
Energy (kJ Cal)	1009 241
Carb (g)	41
Prot (g)	6
Fat (g)	6
Fibre	

Preparation time: 20 minutes
Cooking time: 1 hour 10 minutes

PAUL MILLER ~ boxing
carrot cake
Greatest sporting moment:
Boxing at the 2000 Olympic Games in Sydney.
Favourite Food: sweet chilli hokkien noodles and vegetables.
My contribution to Survival 2:
When making weight leading into a boxing tournament, I have to reduce the quantities of my meals, but I always make room for a small serving of dessert. I find that when I have to limit my food intake, it helps to finish off an evening meal with something sweet.

carrot cake

cinnamon rolls

raspberry pear crumble

cinnamon rolls   Makes 18   ❋

3½ cups plain flour
1 teaspoon salt
2 tablespoons raw sugar
1 tablespoon brown sugar
½ teaspoon cinnamon
7 g sachet dry yeast
1 teaspoon bread improver (optional)
1 teaspoon olive oil
½ cup low-fat milk, at room temperature
¾ cup warm water

Cinnamon filling:
½ cup brown sugar, extra
2 teaspoons cinnamon, extra
1½ cups mixed dry fruit
4 tablespoons margarine

Combine flour, salt, sugars, cinnamon, yeast and bread improver in a large bowl. Make a well in the centre. Add oil, milk and water. Mix with a wooden spoon, then gather dough into a ball and turn out on a lightly floured surface. Knead for 10 minutes, or until dough is smooth, reflouring the surface, if required. Lightly spray a large bowl with oil, and place dough in bowl. Cover with a clean tea towel. Leave in a warm place for 1 hour, until much increased in size. Preheat oven to 180°C (350°F). Lightly grease two large baking trays. Knead dough again on a floured surface for 1 minute. Roll out to a rectangle (36 x 26 cm), about 1-cm thick. Combine filling ingredients and spread over dough, leaving a 2-cm border along one long side. Roll up dough, starting from opposite side to bare edge. Cut in 2-cm slices with a large sharp knife. Arrange slices on trays, close together with 'ends' on the inside so they don't unroll. Bake for 20–25 minutes, until browned. Cool on trays.

ANALYSIS	18
Energy (kJ Cal)	804 192
▨ Carb (g)	36
Prot (g)	4
▨ Fat (g)	4

HINT: *If using a breadmaker, follow manufacturer's instructions for making the dough. Then follow the recipe to make the cinnamon rolls.*

Preparation time:
20 minutes + 1 hour standing
Cooking time: 20-25 minutes

ADAM PINE ~ swimming
raspberry pear crumble
Greatest sporting moment:
Competing in front of a huge crowd at the 2000 Olympics in Sydney.
Favourite part about Survival 1:
The recipes are fast and easy. Sasha (my lovely new wife) made all of them!
My contribution to Survival 2:
This dessert is so good and easy to make. You can eat it hot or cold ... even for breakfast!

raspberry pear crumble   Serves 4-6   ❋

825 g can pear slices in natural juice, drained
300 g frozen or fresh raspberries
1 cup rolled oats
¼ cup desiccated coconut (optional)
½ cup wholemeal plain flour
2 tablespoons brown sugar
2 tablespoons margarine
2 tablespoons golden syrup

Preheat oven to 180°C (350°F). Put pears into a 6-cup capacity ovenproof dish, and spread raspberries over them. Combine oats, coconut, flour and brown sugar in a mixing bowl. Melt margarine and golden syrup together in a small saucepan, then add to flour mixture. Mix until ingredients are evenly moistened. Spread over pear mixture. Bake for 25 minutes or until golden brown.

HINT: *Use 6 small ovenproof bowls to make individual crumbles and bake for 15 minutes. This recipe keeps in the fridge for up to 2 days and can be eaten cold. To reheat, put a serve in an ovenproof bowl and warm in a 180°C (350°F) oven for 10–15 minutes.*

ANALYSIS	4	6
Energy (kJ Cal)	1741 416	1161 277
▨ Carb (g)	77	52
▨ Prot (g)	7	4
▨ Fat (g)	9	6
▨ Fibre		

Preparation time: 10 minutes
Cooking time: 30 minutes

chocolate mousse

chocolate mousse Serves 4-6

1 litre carton low-fat prepared vanilla custard
½ cup NESTLÉ Baking Cocoa
¼ cup icing sugar
3 teaspoons gelatine
2 egg whites

Place custard in a large mixing bowl. Sift in cocoa and sugar. Combine gently, using a wire whisk until smooth. Put 2 tablespoons hot water in a small bowl and sprinkle gelatine over. Stand bowl in a saucepan with about 1–2 cm hot water, and place over low heat for about 1 minute until gelatine has softened. Remove bowl from saucepan and whisk gelatine, using a fork to dissolve. Set aside to cool slightly. Beat egg whites in a clean dry bowl, with clean beaters, until soft peaks form. Add egg whites and gelatine to custard mixture and fold gently until combined. Using a metal spoon or rubber spatula, work carefully so as not to lose the volume from the egg whites. Transfer to a 6-cup capacity serving bowl, or six individual 1-cup bowls. Refrigerate for 2 hours until softly set. Serve with fresh strawberries, if desired.

ANALYSIS	4		6	
Energy (kJ Cal)	1200	287	800	191
■ Carb (g)		48		32
■ Prot (g)		15		10
■ Fat (g)		4		3
■ Calcium				

HINT: *For a special garnish, use a vegetable peeler to make chocolate shavings from a block of NESTLÉ PLAISTOWE Dark Cooking Chocolate, and sprinkle them over the mousse.*

Preparation time:
20 minutes + 2 hours refrigeration
Cooking time: 1 minute

lemon-lime cheesecake Serves 6-8

100 g reduced-fat butternut biscuits
2 tablespoons margarine, melted
250 g reduced-fat cream cheese
1 tablespoon finely grated lemon rind
2 teaspoons finely grated lime rind
400 g can CARNATION Sweetened Condensed Skim Milk
2 tablespoons lemon juice
2 tablespoons lime juice
3 teaspoons gelatine
2 egg whites

Lightly grease a 20-cm round nonstick springform pan. Place biscuits in a food processor and process until finely crushed. Add margarine, and process briefly until evenly moistened. Press crumbs into the base of the pan, smoothing with the back of a spoon. Refrigerate while making the filling. Using electric beaters, beat cream cheese with lemon and lime rind until combined. Add milk and lemon and lime juice, and beat until smooth. Put 1½ tablespoons hot water in a small bowl and sprinkle over gelatine. Stand the bowl in a saucepan with about 1–2 cm hot water, and place over low heat for 1 minute until gelatine has softened. Remove bowl from saucepan and whisk gelatine, using a fork, to dissolve. Set aside to cool slightly. Beat egg whites in a clean dry bowl, with clean beaters, until soft peaks form. Add egg whites and gelatine to cream cheese mixture and fold gently until combined. Using a rubber spatula or metal spoon, work carefully so as not to lose the volume from the egg whites. Pour over the base and refrigerate for 3 hours, until set. Serve with fresh fruit.

ANALYSIS	6		8	
Energy (kJ Cal)	1502	359	1126	269
■ Carb (g)		47		35
■ Prot (g)		13		10
■ Fat (g)		14		10
■ Calcium				

HINT: *For special occasions, top cheesecake with fresh blueberries or raspberries when it is almost set. This recipe keeps in the fridge for 3 days.*

Preparation time:
20 minutes + 3 hours refrigeration
Cooking time: 1 minute

JACKIE GALLAGHER ~ triathlon and AIS head triathlon coach
chocolate mousse
Greatest sporting moments: **Winning World Triathlon Championship (Cleveland, USA) and World Biathlon Championship in 1996 (Ferrera, Italy).**
Favourite food: **Chocolate (KIT KAT Chunky).**
My contribution to Survival 2:
I always finish off the day with something sweet. I really enjoy eating chocolate, so I am always on the lookout for chocolate alternatives. This chocolate mousse is so simple, even I can cook it—and I am not known for my cooking abilities.

lemon-lime cheesecake

quicktreats

apricot-cherry parfait

grilled peaches

hot banana splits

strawberry creams

quick treats

Sometimes hunger hits or a sweet craving strikes and there's no time for cooking or baking. Fortunately, athletes don't have to miss out on quick treats, as there are many ways to prepare satisfying, high-carbohydrate, low-fat snacks in an instant.

Many basic foods such as fruit, custard, yogurt and ice cream can be easily jazzed up into instant treats which look and taste great. With a little imagination, you can turn an ordinary banana into a fantastic split, or transform some fruit and custard into a parfait. Presentation is the key to making impressive quick treats so experiment with different glasses, bowls, plates or cups—it's amazing how appearance can make food more appealing.

Supermarkets offer many products which can form the basis of high-carbohydrate, low-fat treats. Stock your fridge and pantry with some of these, and you'll always have a quick treat on hand.

FRUIT SECTION	Fresh fruit	Fruit salad, grilled or poached fruit
	Dried fruit	Soak in juice to rehydrate
	Puréed fruit	Use as a sauce for ice cream
BREAD & BAKERY SECTION	Fruit buns	Toast and spread with jam and ricotta
	Sponge fingers	Eat with custard or yogurt
	Bread/raisin bread	Make 'fruit toasties' with a sandwich toaster and fruit fillings
BISCUIT SECTION	Reduced-fat biscuits	Crush and sprinkle on ice cream
	Rice cakes	Top with mashed banana, a scoop of ricotta and a sprinkle of cinnamon
DESSERT SECTION	Creamed rice	Add fruit, honey or MILO
	Jelly	Make your own jelly fruit
	Pie fruit	Great for crumbles, fruit toasties and fruit pizzas
	Canned fruit	Serve warm for a change. Add to custard, yogurt, jelly and ice cream. Try different combinations such as pear and berries.
	Jellied fruit	Have on its own or mix with custard and sponge fingers to make a trifle
FRIDGE SECTION	Yogurt	All of these are great on their own or when combined with fruit, sponge fingers, crushed biscuits etc.
	Custard	
	Reduced-fat mousse	
	Dairy snacks/Frûche	
FREEZER SECTION	Low-fat ice cream	Top off any treat
	Frozen fruit dessert	Serve with fruit or jelly
	Light fruit pies	
	Frozen berries	Use in parfaits and trifles

apricot-cherry parfait Serves 4

Divide 1 cup low-fat prepared custard among four 1-cup capacity serving glasses (or bowls). Drain an 825 g can apricot halves. Cut apricots in half again. Divide ⅓ of the apricots among the glasses, then divide a 200 g carton NESTLÉ Light or NESTLÉ Activ Iron & Calcium Black Cherry Yogurt (note Activ will have more calcium and fibre content) among the glasses. Layer half remaining apricots onto the yogurt, then divide another 1 cup low-fat prepared custard among the glasses. Top with remaining apricots and another 200 g carton NESTLÉ Light Yogurt. Crush 4 amaretti biscuits (almond macaroons) in a small bowl, and sprinkle over each parfait.

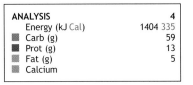

ANALYSIS	4
Energy (kJ Cal)	1404 335
◼ Carb (g)	59
◼ Prot (g)	13
▥ Fat (g)	5
▥ Calcium	

grilled peaches Serves 4

Cut 4 fresh peaches in half and remove the stones. Peel the peaches if you like. Place peaches cut side up in a shallow heatproof dish. Combine 2 tablespoons brown sugar and ½ teaspoon ground cinnamon in a small bowl, then sprinkle over cut surface of the peaches. Cook under a hot grill for 3-4 minutes until sugar is dissolved and bubbling. Serve with PETERS FARM No Fat Natural Yogurt.

ANALYSIS	4
Energy (kJ Cal)	618 148
◼ Carb (g)	28
Prot (g)	7
▥ Fat (g)	<1
▥ Calcium	

hot banana splits Serves 4

Preheat oven to 190°C (375°F). Cut 4 bananas in half lengthways and lay each one on a sheet of aluminium foil. Sprinkle 2 tablespoons NESTLÉ Choc Bits, Dark Chocolate over the surface of banana halves. Bring halves back together and wrap in foil. Place foil parcels on a baking tray. Bake for 10 minutes until chocolate is soft and bananas heated through. Sprinkle with 2 teaspoons crushed peanuts over each split and serve with a scoop of PETERS Light & Creamy Vanilla Ice Cream.

ANALYSIS	4
Energy (kJ Cal)	1234 295
◼ Carb (g)	45
Prot (g)	6
▥ Fat (g)	11

strawberry creams Serves 4

Wash and hull 1 punnet of strawberries, slice thinly, and place in a glass or ceramic bowl. Sprinkle 2 teaspoons caster sugar and 2 tablespoons fresh orange juice over strawberries. Set aside for 10 minutes, then drain, reserving liquid. Stir through 2 x 200 g cartons NESTLÉ Light Strawberries & Cream Yogurt. Transfer to serving glasses and drizzle with some of the reserved liquid. Serve with 1 or 2 sponge fingers (savoyardi biscuits) for dipping, if desired.

ANALYSIS	4
Energy (kJ Cal)	794 190
◼ Carb (g)	36
Prot (g)	8
▥ Fat (g)	1
▥ Vitamin C	
▥ Calcium	

muffins

banana muffin

chocolate choc-chip muffin

ginger pear muffin

orange poppyseed muffin

➤ To maximise time-efficiency, make a double batch of muffins and freeze some (they keep in the freezer for up to 3 months).

➤ Use nonstick muffin tins for best results, but even nonstick tins will need to be slightly greased—spray them lightly with oil.

➤ Don't leave muffins in the tin for too long after baking—give them a couple of minutes to firm up, then run a knife around each muffin and gently ease from the tin. Place muffins on a cake rack to cool completely.

➤ Muffin-sized paper cases are available in the baking section of most supermarkets. Use these if you don't have a muffin tin, or if you want to save on washing up. The foil cases work best.

➤ Muffins can be topped with custard or ice cream to make a quick dessert. Sauces such as canned passionfruit, mango puree or apple sauce can be used to liven up tired muffins.

➤ To keep the fat content of muffins low, use ingredients such as oil, butter, margarine, chocolate, nuts and coconut sparingly.

➤ Canned berries are a great addition to muffin recipes. Include the juice and reduce the other fluids accordingly.

muffins

Muffins have become hugely popular in recent years, partly because of their reputation as a 'healthy' alternative to cakes and biscuits. But while they do have potential to be nutritious high-carbohydrate snacks, the reality is that many muffins are very high in fat and lacking in other nutrients.

The recipes we have included here are low-fat favourites, and taste great—we know because we've seen the rate at which our muffins disappear from the AIS Dining Hall.

Muffins are most appropriate as a snack or sweet treat. While it is popular practice to use muffins as a substitute for breakfast, they really aren't suitable for this purpose. Most muffins are too low in fibre and vitamins and minerals such as calcium to act as a breakfast replacement.

To keep the fat content of muffins low, it's best to make them yourself. They're one of the simplest treats to bake, and even the most basic cook can master muffins. The key is to mix the ingredients by hand, rather than using an electric beater. And, only mix the ingredients until they are just combined—over-mixing makes the muffins tough.

Once you've mastered a basic muffin recipe, experiment to create your own concoctions. Good additions to basic recipes include fresh or canned fruit, dried fruit, mashed or grated vegetables such as pumpkin or zucchini, juice, polenta, nuts, seeds, breakfast cereal, cocoa and jam.

A batch of muffins, hot from the oven, is hard to resist. Once cool, wrap muffins in single-serve airtight bags or containers and pop them in the freezer. This ensures you have a long-term supply of delicious muffins. Remove the muffins from the freezer in the morning and take them with you to school, work or training. By mid-morning, the muffin will be nicely thawed and ready to eat. Alternatively, you can reheat frozen muffins in the microwave oven on HIGH for about 40 seconds.

banana muffin   Serves 12 ❅

1½ cups self-raising flour
1 cup wholemeal self-raising flour
¾ cup brown sugar
2 tablespoons margarine, melted
1 cup (250 ml) skim milk
1 egg
1 teaspoon vanilla essence
2 ripe bananas, well mashed

Preheat oven to 180°C (350°F). Lightly grease a 12-hole muffin pan. Sift flours into a large bowl (tip husks into the bowl, too). Stir in sugar and make a well in the centre. In a small bowl, whisk margarine, milk, egg, vanilla and banana together using a fork, then add to flour mixture. Stir gently until mixture is just combined but do not overbeat. Spoon mixture into prepared pan. Bake for 20–25 minutes or until muffins are well risen and spring back to the touch. Leave in pan for a few minutes, then transfer to a wire rack to cool, or eat warm.

Preparation time: 15 minutes
Cooking time: 25 minutes

ANALYSIS	12
Energy (kJ Cal)	762 182
Carb (g)	34
Prot (g)	5
Fat (g)	3

variations
chocolate choc-chip muffin ❅

Omit the wholemeal flour and increase the self-raising flour to 2½ cups. Add ½ teaspoon bicarbonate of soda and ¼ cup NESTLÉ Baking Cocoa when sifting flour. Replace brown sugar with caster sugar. Omit the banana. Add 1 cup NESTLÉ Choc Bits, Dark Chocolate to dry ingredients before stirring in liquids. Omit vanilla essence, and add 200 g PETERS FARM No Fat Natural Yogurt.

HINT: *Instead of skim milk, you can use 1 cup CARNATION Light and Creamy Evaporated Milk.*

ANALYSIS	12
Energy (kJ Cal)	1085 259
Carb (g)	43
Prot (g)	6
Fat (g)	7

ginger pear muffin ❅

Add 2 teaspoons ground ginger when sifting the flours. Replace the banana with 2 large, ripe pears, peeled and grated. Omit vanilla essence, reduce milk to ¾ cup and add 200 g PETERS FARM No Fat Natural Yogurt. Dust lightly with icing sugar when cool.

ANALYSIS	12
Energy (kJ Cal)	823 197
Carb (g)	37
Prot (g)	5
Fat (g)	3

orange poppyseed muffin ❅

Omit wholemeal flour and increase self-raising flour to 2½ cups. Replace brown sugar with caster sugar. Add 1½ tablespoons poppyseeds with sugar. Omit banana. Add ½ cup orange juice with the milk. Replace vanilla with 1 tablespoon finely grated orange rind.

ANALYSIS	12
Energy (kJ Cal)	716 171
Carb (g)	32
Prot (g)	4
Fat (g)	3

MANUELA BERCHTOLD &
JANE SEXTON ~ freestyle skiing
muffins
Greatest sporting moments:
Manuela—Winning Junior World
Combined Champion 1996,
in Chatel, France.
Jane—Competing in the
2001 World Championships,
Blackcomb, Canada.
Favourite food:
Manuela—Chocolate
and mangoes.
Jane—Cookies, especially white
choc-chip and macadamia.
Contribution to Survival 2:
You can see from our favourites
that we have sweet tooths! For
mogul skiing, we need a good
power-to-weight ratio which
means keeping skinfolds low.
These muffin recipes satisfy
our sweet cravings, without
containing too much fat.

tips for travelling

Travelling can broaden experiences and fill up a passport, but it also presents a new array of eating challenges to athletes. These include disruptions to usual training and eating schedules, changes to food availability, changes in climate, and the excitement and distractions of a new environment. The following ideas will help you to take your winning diet with you, wherever you go.

Plan Ahead

- Contact the airline to find out what meal services will be provided. Sometimes you may want to arrange special meals suited to your requirements (this must be done well in advance). Check what is in the 'athlete's meals', 'low-fat meals' or 'vegetarian meals' on offer as sometimes these are not what they seem.
- Investigate the availability of food at your destination as thoroughly as possible before leaving home. Try to find out the location of shops and restaurants and their opening hours, as well as the self-catering or food storage facilities at your accommodation.
- Find out your daily schedule so that you can plan meals around this. Often, training or competitions will clash with your normal meal and snack times, and a new or flexible food schedule will be needed.
- With this information, make a general plan of where, when and what you will eat. Try to stick to your usual meal pattern as much as possible while away, but be prepared for any changes.
- Take your own food or snacks to replace the key items you may not be able to find at your destination (see list).
- Carry a selection of snack foods with you at all times. Do not let yourself get too hungry or you are likely to be tempted by the first fast-food outlet you see.

USEFUL FOOD FOR TRAVELLING
■ cereal bars
■ breakfast cereal + powdered milk
■ snack-pack fruits
■ dried fruits
■ MAGGI 2-Minute Fat Free Noodles
■ rice cakes
■ jam, honey, peanut butter, Vegemite™
■ powdered sports drink
■ powdered liquid meal supplements
■ baked beans, canned spaghetti
■ packets of instant pasta in sauce

Eat and Drink Well When on the Move

The unglamorous part of travel is having to sit still for long periods. Forced inactivity, increased fluid loss, low-fibre diets and changes in time zone can lead to increased dehydration and sluggish digestion. This may interfere with your performance for the first few days after arrival, but, on tours where you are constantly on the road, it can become a significant chronic problem. Boredom eating while inactive can also add up to unwanted weight gain.

- Planes are particularly dehydrating, but fluid loss can also increase in airconditioned buses or hot environments. You will need to drink regularly to counteract this loss. Carry a water bottle with you on trips and drink to your own schedule rather than when beverage services are available.
- Avoid alcohol on planes, and be wary of relying only on fluids containing caffeine (tea, coffee, cola drinks) to keep hydrated. Water, mineral water, juices, soft drinks or sports drinks are the best fluid choices.
- Don't confuse boredom with hunger. Plan your food intake in advance and decide which meals you need, and whether your own snacks are also required. Stick to this plan. Don't be tempted by all the meal services offered on plane flights, or the shops visited during stops on bus trips.
- On long-haul flights, adopt the meal pattern that you will have at your destination—for example, accept only the meals that coincide with breakfast and dinner times at

your new location. This might see you sleeping through some of the plane meals, but, as well as benefiting from extra sleep, you will speed up the adjustment of your body clock.

- Carry some higher fibre snacks (wholemeal breakfast bars or dried fruit) if you suffer from constipation on long journeys and keep well hydrated.
- Chew sugar-free gum to clean your teeth and stop you from boredom snacking.

Be Wary of Food and Water Hygiene

Many countries have lower standards of hygiene and water purity than we enjoy, and the resulting gastric reactions can cause a major impairment of performance as well as spoil the fun of overseas travel.

- Find out whether it is safe to drink the local water supply. If it isn't, keep to bottled water or drinks served in sealed containers. Be wary of ice added to drinks in case it is made from tap water, and even clean your teeth using your bottled water supplies. Some athletes stick to these rules in all new environments, at least for the first few days.
- In high-risk environments, keep to food served in the restaurants of good hotels, or well-known food franchises. Avoid eating food from street stalls and local markets, however inviting and authentic it seems. You should also avoid fruit, unless it can be peeled, and fresh salads. Only eat foods that are well cooked and be wary of local seafood and ice cream.

Use Takeaway Food Well

Takeaway food can be a cheap and convenient option while travelling. Often, takeaway outlets are the only shops open, or the cleanest and safest food supplier. Although many takeaway food choices are high in fat and low on fuel, there are still good choices to be made. In general, look for chains or outlets that let you make you own order instead of those which serve standard products. Salad bars are ideal, but avoid 'meal deals' which, although cheap, see you eating extra fries or fatty desserts that you don't really need. Good choices are:

- bread rolls or sandwiches with plenty of salad, lean meat fillings and no margarine
- pizza—choose thick-crust varieties and vegetarian or lean-meat toppings, and ask for less cheese
- hamburgers—make sure they are grilled and have plenty of salad added. Choose tomato sauce rather than mayonnaise or creamy dressings, and avoid extras such as double meat, fried eggs, bacon or cheese
- Asian food—make steamed rice the meal base and add stirfries with vegetables and lean meats. Avoid battered and deep-fried dishes, including most appetisers
- Mexican—fajitas (corn tortillas around grilled beef, chicken or seafood) and rice, salad and salsa. Avoid excessive cheese and sour cream
- souvlaki
- baked potato—avoid butter and sour cream
- hearty vegetable-filled soups with bread
- low-fat smoothies
- low-fat frozen yogurt with fruit toppings or fruit salad
- fresh fruit
- plain mineral water or juices
- skim milk hot chocolate or cappuccino

Restaurant Eating

Although restaurants can be expensive when you are on a budget, you may find yourself in a situation where you can cater for your own breakfasts and lunches and eat out in the evenings. Most restaurants provide a varied menu that caters for high-carbohydrate low-fat eating, although you may need to make some special requests.

- Make sure that your water glass is topped up regularly to help with hydration goals. For extra carbohydrate, soft drinks or fruit juice may also be good.
- Choose meals that focus on carbohydrate choices such as rice or pasta. With pasta, go for tomato-based sauces rather than cream-based sauces. Risotto or paella also make good choices as long as there is not too much oil used in the cooking.
- Asian food offers lots of possibilities. Fill your plate or bowl with steamed rice or plain noodles and choose a main dish based on lean meat, fish or chicken, and plenty of vegetables. Avoid dishes that are deep-fried or battered.
- If you are having a main course based on meat, fish or poultry, choose a medium-sized portion and don't forget the fuel foods such as a baked potato or a side dish of rice. Get the bread basket topped up.
- Order side serves of vegetables or salad if they don't come with the meal. Ask for black pepper, tomato sauce or salsa rather than buttery sauces, and lemon juice rather than oil-based salad dressings.
- Carbohydrate-rich desserts include rice pudding, bread and butter pudding, sorbet, fruit salad or fruit crumble. If you're watching your total energy intake, finish up with a fruit platter or skim milk hot chocolate.

Planning Ahead to Look After a Team

Feeding a sporting team can be a logistical nightmare, especially when events finish late at night. It can be sometimes hard for restaurants to handle large numbers and individual meal requests quickly.

- Book a restaurant ahead of time and negotiate a menu. It also helps to ring ahead to fine-tune your arrival time so that food will be ready as you walk in the door.
- Buffet eating is recommended—it's quick for hungry athletes, cost-saving when negotiating prices with the restaurant and offers flexibility so that each athlete can choose the type and amount of food that they need.
- Plan a menu based on carbohydrate-rich dishes and offer sufficient choice to meet the preferences of the majority of your athletes. Note that too much choice encourages overeating, because people try a little bit of everything. If you are away for more than a week, put effort into increasing the variety from day to day, rather than within the same meal.
- Make separate arrangements for athletes with special needs (i.e. vegetarians or those with food intolerances). It is hard to accommodate all needs within one menu, so be prepared to arrange for special needs as required.
- Remember that snacks are part of the dietary plan and often neglected when catering arrangements provide for three meals a day. Provide items at meals that can be taken away for eating later—for example, fruit, cartons of yogurt, muffins and breakfast bars. Alternatively, organise a communal room with a fridge so you have somewhere to put these snack items and other choices such as breakfast cereal.

self-catering

Many small groups or individuals choose to stay in apartments and do their own cooking when away on trips. This can be an economical choice that offers flexibility with meal times and food selections.

However, just as with cooking at home, it can be hard to have the motivation and appetite to prepare a meal when you are exhausted from your event or training, and there are added problems with organising menus for limited stays. It is also hard to coordinate dishes that can be made from a limited number of ingredients, and often you end up with leftovers or leftover ingredients or find that your favourite dish doesn't taste the same without that pinch of something you don't have.

Quick and easy meals that require a minimum number of ingredients and equipment are essential, and the following menus solve these difficulties. Firstly, we have provided a full menu plan for a week, in which meal selections are balanced and coordinated to use up all the leftovers. The second menu plan caters for evening meals only, and mixes and matches the recipes so that all ingredients are used. For both plans we've included a shopping list of all the things you need.

Notes on the Shopping Lists
- If you need to save lots of time, contact the local supermarket at your destination and ask if they will collect and deliver your shopping needs. Fax your shopping list in advance of your trip, and arrange for the items to be delivered shortly before or after your arrival.
- Note that some ingredients can be purchased later in the week to provide fresh food and more space in the fridge. These ingredients are marked with an asterix★ in the Shopping List and can be purchased on about Day 4.
- Snacks vary according to the individual and while we have included some snack ideas, you should add them to the list according to your requirements.
- Take advantage of local or seasonal produce, such as fresh fruit and vegetables or bread, at your destination and adjust the Shopping List accordingly.
- Under 'Miscellaneous' in the Shopping List are many foods (like honey and hot drinks) that you should choose according to individual preferences. The sauces, seasonings or herbs may be purchased new with the other supplies, or you may like to take your own. These can be placed in little jars, plastic bags or tubes (such as clean film canisters) and then the whole lot packed into a larger airtight container. You can also leave some of the sauces out of the recipes, or substitute according to what's available.

seven-day menu plan

This menu plan will provide four athletes with three meals per day (breakfast, lunch and dinner) for a week. The recipes are marked with the page numbers for easy reference.

All you have to do is:
- Check the Menu Plan (making any adjustments for special preferences and for the individual items such as snacks).
- If possible, check the availability of cooking equipment in your apartment. You may need to adjust the recipes if important cooking equipment is missing. Alternatively, you can take a time-saving or versatile piece of cooking equipment with you.
- Pack your *Survival from the Fittest* cookbook.
- Follow the Shopping List and buy the ingredients.

Equipment
- stove top
- oven
- nonstick frying pan or wok
- large saucepans
- ovenproof dish or baking tray
- microwave
- microwave dishes
- wooden spoon or large plastic spoons

RECIPE FOR BIRCHER MUSELI
2 cups rolled oats
200 g carton NESTLÉ Light Strawberries & Cream (or Black Cherry) Yogurt
150 ml low-fat milk
$1/2$ cup sultanas
150 ml orange juice
1 punnet strawberries

Soak oats overnight with berry-flavoured yogurt, low-fat milk, sultanas and orange juice. Before serving, cut strawberries, or any other berries you desire, and stir through.

---

shopping list

Bread
- [ ] 4 loaves bread (can include some fruit loaf)
- [ ] 8 slices ciabbata★
- [ ] pack of 10 burrito tortillas
- [ ] 10 bread rolls
- [ ] 10 bread rolls★
- [ ] 3 loaves bread★

Fruit & Vegetables
- [ ] 12 bananas
- [ ] 12 bananas★
- [ ] 10 apples
- [ ] 10 oranges
- [ ] 2 punnets strawberries
- [ ] 4 peaches
- [ ] 2 lemons
- [ ] 10 tomatoes
- [ ] 3 Lebanese cucumbers
- [ ] 2 lettuces
- [ ] salad ingredients (lettuce, tomatoes, carrot, cucumber)★
- [ ] 3 heads of broccoli
- [ ] bunch baby bok choy
- [ ] 400 g button mushrooms
- [ ] bunch asparagus
- [ ] 200 g snow peas
- [ ] 3 carrots
- [ ] 3 red capsicums
- [ ] 2 leeks
- [ ] 2 celery sticks
- [ ] bunch basil★
- [ ] bunch flat-leaf (Italian) parsley
- [ ] 5 onions + 1 red onion
- [ ] bunch spring onions
- [ ] 1 sweet potato
- [ ] 1 sweet potato
- [ ] alfalfa sprouts
- [ ] chives
- [ ] coriander
- [ ] flat-leaf parsley
- [ ] ginger
- [ ] snow pea sprouts

Dairy & Refrigerated Products
- [ ] 4 litres reduced-fat milk
- [ ] 1 litre reduced-fat milk★
- [ ] 2 x 1 kg of NESTLÉ Light Fruit Yogurt of your choice
- [ ] 3 x 1 kg of NESTLÉ Light Swiss Vanilla Yogurt
- [ ] 600 ml low-fat custard
- [ ] 1 kg grated reduced-fat cheese
- [ ] 1 x tub canola-based margarine
- [ ] 2 x 375 g packets fresh lasagne sheets
- [ ] 900 g hokkien noodles
- [ ] 2 large pizza bases (covered in tomato paste)
- [ ] 8 litres orange juice

Meat & Eggs
- [ ] 500 g rump steak
- [ ] 800 g chicken breast fillets
- [ ] 4 fillet steaks★
- [ ] 500 g lean chicken mince
- [ ] 3 barbecued chickens
- [ ] 500 g lean pork fillets★
- [ ] 500 g sliced lean ham
- [ ] 6 eggs

Canned & Packet Goods
- [ ] 2 x 500 g packets breakfast cereal
- [ ] large packet natural muesli
- [ ] 500 g jasmine rice
- [ ] 1 kg arborio rice
- [ ] 2 x 500 g packets penne pasta
- [ ] 4 x 300 g cans butter beans
- [ ] 2 x 450 g cans refried beans
- [ ] 4 x 425 g cans Mexican chilli beans
- [ ] 450 g can tomato soup
- [ ] 4 x 450 g cans beetroot
- [ ] 4 x 450 g cans tuna in springwater/brine
- [ ] 3 x 450 g cans baked beans
- [ ] 2 x 440 g cans corn kernels
- [ ] 2 x 575 g jars tomato-based pasta sauce
- [ ] small jar tomato paste
- [ ] small jar capers
- [ ] plum sauce
- [ ] MAGGI Extra Hot Chilli Sauce
- [ ] 2 x 375 g jars enchilada sauce
- [ ] soy sauce
- [ ] MAGGI Oyster Sauce
- [ ] jar minced garlic
- [ ] 2 x 1 litre cartons MAGGI All Natural Chicken Liquid Stock
- [ ] olive or canola oil spray
- [ ] balsamic vinegar
- [ ] black pepper
- [ ] cinnamon
- [ ] 500 g packet plain wholemeal flour
- [ ] small packet brown sugar
- [ ] packet rolled oats
- [ ] 325 g packet pancake mix
- [ ] 450 g packet sultanas
- [ ] 100 g blanched almonds, chopped
- [ ] 250 g packet sponge fingers
- [ ] 425 g can boysenberries
- [ ] 2 x 425 g can raspberries
- [ ] 2 x 450 g cans sliced mango
- [ ] 170 g can passionfruit pulp
- [ ] 825 g can pear slices
- [ ] 2 x 420 g cans fruit in natural juice
- [ ] 2 x 375 ml CARNATION Light and Creamy Evaporated Milk

Frozen Items
- [ ] 500 g frozen stirfry vegetables
- [ ] 2 litres PETERS Light & Creamy Ice Cream
- [ ] 300 g frozen raspberries

Miscellaneous
- [ ] 500 g honey
- [ ] 500 g jam
- [ ] golden syrup
- [ ] Vegemite™
- [ ] tea
- [ ] coffee
- [ ] drinking chocolate or MILO
- [ ] desiccated coconut
- [ ] chilli powder
- [ ] tomato sauce

Snack Ideas
- [ ] cereal bars
- [ ] English muffins or crumpets
- [ ] dry biscuits
- [ ] salsa or low-fat dips
- [ ] fresh fruit
- [ ] rice cakes

MEAL	DAY 1	DAY 2	DAY 3	DAY 4	DAY 5	DAY 6	DAY 7
Breakfast	Cereal, milk, tinned fruit, NESTLÉ Light or Diet Fruit Yogurt / orange juice	Cereal, milk, tinned fruit, NESTLÉ Light or Diet Fruit Yogurt / orange juice	Bircher Muesli (page 118) (make double quantity)	Cereal, milk, tinned fruit, NESTLÉ Light or Diet Fruit Yogurt / orange juice	Cereal, milk, tinned fruit, NESTLÉ Light or Diet Fruit Yogurt / orange juice	Baked beans, toast	Pancakes (made from packet mix), raspberries/boysenberries (canned), NESTLÉ Light or Diet Fruit Yogurt
Lunch	Salad sandwiches with ham and barbecued chicken / fresh fruit (apples/oranges)	Salad sandwiches with ham and barbecue chicken / fresh fruit (apples/oranges)	Chicken, corn & chive risotto (leftover from Day 1), salad / fresh fruit	Salad sandwiches with ham and tuna / fresh fruit (apples/oranges)	Steak sandwiches (page 92)	Salad sandwiches with tuna and barbecued chicken / fresh fruit (apples/oranges)	B's penne with butter beans & tuna (leftover from Day 5)
Dinner	Chicken, corn & chive risotto (make double quantity) (page 39)	Make trifle first. Gonzo's baked bean burritos (page 26) (make double quantities of burrito mix)	Mary's peppered beef & vegetables (page 71)	Petria's mexican chicken cannelloni (using burrito mix from Day 2) (page 59)	B's penne with butter beans & tuna (make double quantity) (page 56)	Pork with spicy plum sauce (page 80)	Pizza night: Sweet potato, chicken and banana pizza (use leftover vegetables) (page 95)
Accompaniments	Salad	Salad	Rice	Salad	Salad	Salad	Salad and bread
Dessert	Tinned fruit, NESTLÉ Light or Diet Fruit Yogurt, honey and banana	Tropical trifle (page 104) Soak Bircher Muesli for tomorrow	Grilled peaches (page 112) with NESTLÉ Light or Diet Fruit Yogurt	Raspberry pear crumble (page 107) with PETERS Light & Creamy Ice Cream	Tinned fruit, NESTLÉ Light or Diet Fruit Yogurt, honey and banana	Banana with PETERS Light & Creamy Ice Cream	Bircher Muesli warm in microwave (from Day 3)

quick & easy dinner menu

If a less structured approach to meals fits in better with the group, then the Quick & Easy Dinner Menu is ideal. Breakfast can be taken care of with cereal, fruit and toast, while lunch could include sandwiches, toasted sandwiches, yogurt, fruit or leftovers from dinner.

This menu has been modified for quick and easy cooking, as well as including different cooking styles and flavours that require minimal preparation.

Desserts are all taken from the Quick Treats section of this cookbook, or are prepared items from the supermarket.

The recipes have been adapted to be quick, use up all the ingredients you've bought and please a crowd!

All you have to do is:
- Check that the recipe suggestions suit your needs and make alterations as necessary.
- If possible, check what cooking equipment is available at your accommodation.
- Do the shopping from the list.
- Pack *Survival from the Fittest*.

DAY	DINNER	DESSERT
1	Chicken & Noodle Salad	Strawberry Creams
2	Easy Sweet & Sour Pork	Canned fruit, yogurt, honey and banana
3	Speedy Fried Rice	Apricot-Cherry Parfaits
4	Chilli Beef & Vegetable Pasta	Canned fruit, yogurt, honey and banana
5	Pasta with Chicken & Sundried Tomato	Rice pudding (pre-prepared) and canned mango slices
6	Quick Lentil Burgers	Canned fruit, yogurt, honey and banana
7	Pizza	Hot Banana Splits

shopping list

Bread
- ☐ 4 wholemeal hamburger buns

Fruit & Vegetables
- ☐ cos lettuce
- ☐ punnet cherry tomatoes
- ☐ bunch spring onions
- ☐ Lebanese cucumber
- ☐ 1 carrot
- ☐ 400 g button mushrooms
- ☐ 5 red capsicums + 2 green capsicums
- ☐ 80 g baby English spinach leaves
- ☐ salad ingredients (tomato, lettuce, cucumber, avocado)
- ☐ 1 lime
- ☐ bunch coriander
- ☐ 2 onions
- ☐ 200 g potatoes
- ☐ 300 g sundried tomatoes
- ☐ 8 bananas
- ☐ 8 bananas★
- ☐ punnet strawberries
- ☐ 1 orange
- ☐ 2 small mangoes

Dairy & Refrigerated Products
- ☐ 900 g hokkien noodles
- ☐ ½ dozen eggs
- ☐ 500 g reduced-fat tasty cheese
- ☐ 2 large pizza bases (spread with tomato paste)
- ☐ 1 litre carton low-fat custard
- ☐ 2 x 200 g carton of NESTLÉ Light Black Cherry Yogurt
- ☐ 1 x 1 kg carton of NESTLÉ Light Strawberries & Cream Yogurt
- ☐ 1 x 1 kg carton of NESTLÉ Light Swiss Vanilla Yogurt

Meat
- ☐ 3 barbecued chickens
- ☐ 150 g shaved reduced-fat ham
- ☐ 500 g lean pork fillets
- ☐ 500 g lean beef mince★

Canned & Packet Goods
- ☐ olive or canola oil spray
- ☐ MAGGI Fish Sauce
- ☐ MAGGI Soy Sauce
- ☐ MAGGI Chilli Sauce
- ☐ 500 ml MAGGI All Natural Beef Liquid Stock
- ☐ minced garlic
- ☐ 575 g jar of tomato-based pasta sauce
- ☐ 440 g can red kidney beans
- ☐ 1 kg jasmine rice
- ☐ 2 x 400 g cans green lentils
- ☐ 2 x 40 g packets sesame seeds
- ☐ 100 g packet chopped almonds
- ☐ 100 g crushed peanuts
- ☐ 250 g packet breadcrumbs
- ☐ 500 g pasta (e.g. spirals or bows)
- ☐ 500 g spaghetti
- ☐ NESTLÉ Choc Bits, Dark chocolate
- ☐ 825 g can apricot halves
- ☐ 440 g can pineapple pieces
- ☐ amaretti biscuits
- ☐ savoyardi (sponge finger) biscuits
- ☐ caster sugar
- ☐ 4 x 440 g cans Rice Cream
- ☐ 425 g can sliced mango
- ☐ honey

Frozen Items
- ☐ 500 g packet frozen vegetables (peas, corn and carrot)
- ☐ 1 litre PETERS Light & Creamy Ice cream or 1 litre frozen sorbet or fruit dessert★

Miscellaneous
- ☐ ground black pepper
- ☐ oil-free salad dressing

DAY 1
chicken & noodle salad

900 g hokkien noodles

500 g barbecued chicken

1 small cos lettuce, leaves torn

1 punnet cherry tomatoes, quartered

4 spring onions, sliced diagonally

1 Lebanese cucumber, halved lengthways and sliced

2 small mangoes, chopped

2 tablespoons lime or lemon juice

2 tablespoons MAGGI Fish Sauce

1 tablespoon MAGGI Soy Sauce

2 tablespoons MAGGI Chilli Sauce

$^1/_3$ cup coriander leaves

2 tablespoons crushed peanuts, optional

Place noodles in a large heatproof bowl and cover with boiling water. Leave to stand for 2 minutes, stirring gently with a wooden spoon to separate strands. Drain well and set aside. Remove all skin and fat from chicken, and cut meat into strips. Place chicken, noodles, lettuce, tomato, spring onion, cucumber and mango in a mixing bowl. In a small bowl or jug, mix lime juice and sauces. Pour over the noodle salad and toss well to combine. Serve sprinkled with coriander leaves and peanuts.

Serve Strawberry Creams for dessert (see Quick Treats, page 112, for recipe).

DAY 2
easy sweet & sour pork ✳

3 cups white long-grain rice

440 g can pineapple pieces, drained,
reserve 1 tablespoon juice

575 g jar tomato-based pasta sauce

1 tablespoon MAGGI Chilli Sauce

olive or canola oil spray

500 g lean pork fillet, cut into thin strips

1 onion, sliced

1 small red capsicum, chopped

1 small green capsicum, chopped

1 carrot, thinly sliced

1 teaspoon minced garlic

Cook rice in a large saucepan of boiling water for about 12 minutes or until tender; drain well and keep warm. Meanwhile, combine reserved pineapple juice with $^1/_4$ cup pasta sauce, and the chilli sauce. Spray a nonstick wok or frying pan with oil and heat. Stirfry pork in batches over high heat for 2–3 minutes until browned. Set aside. Reheat wok, add onion, capsicum and carrot and stirfry over high heat for 3 minutes until just soft. Add garlic and stirfry for 30 seconds. Add sauce mixture and pineapple pieces to wok, then pork. Stir until heated through. Serve with half the cooked rice (and save remaining for fried rice).

HINT: *The rest of the jar of pasta sauce is used in the recipe for Day 4.*

Serve canned fruit, yogurt, honey and banana for dessert.

DAY 3
speedy fried rice ✳

olive or canola oil spray

2 eggs, lightly beaten

2 spring onions, sliced

1 red capsicum, chopped

1 cup frozen mixed vegetables (peas, corn and carrots)

150 g shaved reduced-fat ham, chopped

4 cups cooked cold rice (leftover from Day 2)

2 tablespoons MAGGI Soy Sauce

1 tablespoon MAGGI Chilli Sauce

Spray a large nonstick frying pan or wok with oil and heat. Pour in the egg and swirl wok so that egg evenly covers the base and sides. Cook over low–medium heat until set. Turn and cook the other side. Remove from wok, cool slightly, then roll up and cut into thin shreds. Spray wok again and stirfry spring onion over medium heat for 1–2 minutes until soft. Add vegetables and stirfry until tender. Add ham, rice and egg, and stir until heated through. Stir in sauces and serve.

Serve Apricot-Cherry Parfaits for dessert (see Quick Treats, page 112, for recipe).

DAY 4
chilli beef & vegetable pasta ✳

olive or canola oil spray
500 g premium lean beef mince
2 tablespoons MAGGI Chilli Sauce
1 cup (250 ml) MAGGI All Natural Beef Liquid Stock
remainder of 575 g jar tomato-based pasta sauce
440 g can red kidney beans, rinsed and drained
1/2 cup frozen vegetables (peas, corn & carrots)
1 small green capsicum, diced
500 g spaghetti

Spray a large saucepan with oil and heat. Add mince and cook over high heat for about 5 minutes, until browned, using a fork to break up the lumps. Stir in chilli sauce, stock and pasta sauce, and bring to the boil. Reduce heat to low and simmer, partially covered, for 15 minutes, stirring occasionally. Add beans and vegetables and cook for 5 minutes. Meanwhile, cook pasta in a large saucepan of boiling water until al dente. Drain and serve with sauce.

Serve canned fruit, yogurt, honey and banana for dessert.

DAY 5
pasta with chicken & sundried tomato ✳

500 g pasta (e.g. spirals or bows)
olive or canola oil spray
1 red capsicum, sliced lengthways
100 g button mushrooms, sliced
2 teaspoons minced garlic
100 g sundried tomatoes, drained
500 g barbecued chicken
80 g baby English spinach leaves
4 tablespoons reduced-fat tasty cheese
freshly ground black pepper, to taste

Start cooking pasta in a large saucepan of boiling water. Meanwhile, spray a nonstick frying pan with oil and heat. Add capsicum, mushrooms and garlic and stirfry for 1 minute, then add sundried tomatoes and chicken. Cook for 2 minutes until just soft. Drain pasta and return to the saucepan. Add spinach leaves and cheese and toss until combined. Season with black pepper.

HINT: *Use dry sundried tomatoes, available in the fruit and vegetable section at the supermarket, rather than those presoaked in jars of oil.*

Serve rice pudding and canned mango slices for dessert.

DAY 6
quick lentil burgers ✳

Lentil patties:
2 x 440 g cans green lentils, drained
1 cup cooked potato
1/4 cup sesame seeds
1/2 cup finely chopped almonds
1 cup dried breadcrumbs
1 egg, lightly beaten

olive or canola oil spray
4 wholemeal buns, lightly toasted
mixed salad, to serve
MAGGI Chilli Sauce, to serve

Place lentils in a large mixing bowl and add potato. Mash together well, then add sesame seeds, almonds, breadcrumbs and egg. Mix until well combined. Divide into portions and shape into patties. Spray a nonstick frying pan with oil and heat. Cook patties over medium heat for 5 minutes on each side or until golden brown. Serve the patties on wholemeal buns, with salad and sweet chilli sauce to taste.

HINT: *These patties can also be barbecued.*

Serve canned fruit, yogurt, honey and banana for dessert.

DAY 7
pizza

2 large pizza bases (spread with tomato paste)
2 teaspoons minced garlic
1 large onion, chopped
2 handfuls reduced-fat grated cheese

Topping ingredients:
Use leftovers such as sundried tomatoes, barbecue chicken, capsicums and mushrooms

Preheat oven to 180°C (350°F). Place pizza bases on a baking tray and top with garlic, onion, leftover toppings and cheese. Bake for 20 minutes, until the base is crisp and golden and the cheese is melted.

Serve Hot Banana Splits for dessert (see Quick Treats, page 112, for recipe).

making sense of food labels

Many convenience foods are great as shortcuts or for easy meal preparation, but it can be hard to identify which of the vast array of foods in the supermarket belongs in your shopping trolley. Fortunately, many products provide nutrition information on their labels and these can help to make your decision easier. Nutrition information panels are set out in the following way.

NUTRITION INFORMATION SERVINGS PER PACK: 1 SERVING SIZE: 150 g		
	PER SERVE	PER 100 g
ENERGY	618 kJ	412 kJ
PROTEIN	7.8 g	5.2 g
FAT	0.6 g	0.4 g
CARBOHYDRATE		
- TOTAL	27.3 g	18.2 g
- SUGARS	27.3 g	18.2 g
SODIUM	93 mg	62 mg
CALCIUM	411 mg	274 mg
POTASSIUM	330 mg	220 mg

This panel summarises the content of some important nutrients in a food product. These details are provided per 100 g of the food (which makes it easy to compare with other foods), and per 'serve' (take into account this serve may be quite different from the amount you eat). Use the information to gauge how your anticipated serve of food will contribute to your nutrition goals. For example, will it help you to meet your daily target of 800 mg of calcium? Is this food a good choice to fit within your daily fat budget? How much would you have to eat to get 50 g of carbohydrate?

There are many claims on products which sound enticing but they can be misleading. Watch out for some of the following and understand what they really mean:

- REDUCED-FAT ~ The product contains less fat than the original version (usually 25 per cent less). It is not necessarily low in fat. For example, reduced-fat cheese is still a high-fat food.
- LOW-FAT~According to Australian Food Regulations, products may only be labelled low-fat if they contain less than a specified amount of fat. Any product labelled in this way is worth looking at.
- LITE OR LIGHT~However it is spelt, this is a claim that requires further investigation. Lite or Light can refer to colour, flavour, salt or fat. Check the nutrition information panel.
- LOW-CHOLESTEROL ~ Low-cholesterol products are not always low in fat. Check the fat content on the nutrition information panel.
- OVEN-BAKED ~ These products may be 'baked not fried' but they can still be very high in fat.
- ALL NATURAL~Being natural does not always mean the food is good for you. Fat is natural but not desirable in large quantities. Check the nutrition information panel.
- 90% FAT-FREE ~ Means the product contains 10 per cent fat. It does not mean the food contains 90% less fat.

Unfortunately, it is the less nutritious products on the market that tend not to provide a nutrition information panel, but you can still get a feel for the product by examining the ingredient list. Ingredients are listed in order of quantity, starting with the greatest amounts. As a general guide, foods with a fat source as one of the first two or three ingredients are usually not great choices, and should be eaten in small amounts or less regularly. The following table will help you recognise some of the sources of fat, fibre or carbohydrate, and also some of their other names.

FAT	CARBOHYDRATE	FIBRE
Vegetable oil	Glucose	Oats
Copha	Maltose	Cereal
Milk solids	Sucrose	Bran
Palm oil	Glucose syrup	NSP
Shortening	Maltodextrin	Rice
Cocoa butter	Dextrose	
Cream	Juice concentrate	

PERCENTAGE OF FAT

Food manufacturers discuss percentages according to the weight (mass) of the ingredient or nutrient. A food product with 10 per cent fat contains 10 per cent of its mass as fat. However, nutritionists are also interested in the proportion of kilojoules this represents. Ten per cent fat by weight does not mean 10 per cent of energy or kilojoules. After all, fat, protein and carbohydrate provide different energy values, and the water content of a food can distort the kilojoule to mass ratio.

In our recipes, we have stated the energy value of the food, but you can easily calculate the percentage of energy provided by a nutrient in the products you buy using the following method:

- Read the food label to find the quantity (by gram weight) of the nutrient in a serve.
- Multiply grams of fat by 37, grams of carbohydrate by 16, and grams of protein by 17.
- Divide this number by the kilojoule value of the same portion of the food, multiply by 100, and you have the percentage of energy provided by the nutrient.

glossary & conversions

conversions

Liquid Measures

20 ml	= 1 tablespoon	
60 ml	= 1/4 cup	= 2 fl oz
80 ml	= 1/3 cup	= 2¾ fl oz
125 ml	= 1/2 cup	= 4 fl oz
250 ml	= 1 cup	= 8 fl oz
1 litre	= 4 cups	= 32 fl oz

Weight Measures

15 g	= 1/2 oz
30 g	= 1 oz
250 g	= 1/2 lb
500 g	= 1 lb

Length Measures

2.5 mm	= 1/8 inch
5 mm	= 1/4 inch
1 cm	= 1/2 inch
2 cm	= 3/4 inch
2.5 cm	= 1 inch

Oven Temperatures

	°C	°F	Gas Mark
Very Slow	120	250	1/2
Slow	150	300	2
Warm (moderately slow)	160	315	2–3
Moderate	180	350	4
Moderately Hot	190	375	5
Hot	210	415	6–7
Very Hot	230	450	8

glossary

al dente
The cooked texture of pasta when it's ready to eat. Means just firm to the bite.

baking
To cook by dry heat in an oven.

baste
To spoon hot liquid over food as it cooks.

blanch
Place in boiling water for a short time, then plunge into cold water.

crouton
Small cube of fried bread or potato; accompaniment to soups and salads.

dice
Cut into small cubes.

garnish
To decorate, improve the appearance of the dish.

grilling
To cook using dry heat either under an open grill or on a grill plate.

marinate
To soak raw foods in an aromatic liquid to increase the tenderness and impart flavour.

poach
To cook in water or seasoned liquid in an open pan at simmering point with just enough liquid to cover the food.

purée
To mash and sieve food into a smooth consistency.

sauté
To fry briskly using a small amount of oil in a shallow frying pan over moderately high heat. The food is turned or tossed for even browning.

simmer
To keep a liquid at just below boiling point so that only small bubbles rise to the surface.

spray oil
Olive or canola oil available in a spray can.

steam
To cook by vapour from boiling water.

zest
The coloured, oily outer skins of citrus fruit.

index